VAN GOGH AND IMPRESSIONIST PAINTINGS

Grayscale Coloring Book

Enjoy Creating Your Own Work of Art
Creative Grayscale Coloring Book for Relaxation

Volume 2

Iza Bella Art Therapy

USA

I0465728

ABOUT THE BOOK AND COLORING TIPS

The 53 grayscale images of the book have been created from beautiful paintings of famous artists, such as *Monet, Renoir, Degas, Manet, Cézanne, Cassatt, Caillebotte, van Gogh, Gauguin, Lautrec* and *Signac*. Enjoy coloring grayscale pictures of these unique impressionist and postimpressionist masterpieces and create your own work of art. In order to make a masterpiece, simply follow the brush strokes and color over the shades of gray to bring the marvelous painting back to life.

By doing so, you will inspire and contribute to a new artistic movement of 21st century creative colorists. Welcome to the club, we live to create and inspire vibrant colorful life! Creative coloring is freedom, happiness, joy and fun – all at the same time. It is a new way of artistic self-expression and a rewarding personal journey of discovering inner serenity, serendipity and peace.

This grayscale coloring book is suitable for different kinds of colored pencils, markers, pens (chalk pastels for backgrounds, chalk pens, gel pens for highlighting the eyes, crayons, etc). Feel free to experiment with them in order to maximize the fun of your creative experience and enjoy the spontaneous artistic venture itself without being worried about the outcome. If you are like me and you don't always love to color within the lines, then watercoloring will definitely set you free.

Be gentle, wet media, such as watercolor brush pens and aquarellable pencils can cause the paper to buckle, when used over large areas with a lot of water. So I recommend caution especially when applying water. Feel free to choose another media in order to prevent frustration. If you opt for colored pencils and you want to blend strokes nicely, dip the tip of the pencil in petroleum jelly. This will enable the colored tip to glide smoothly across the surface while coloring and it will create a unique even look at the end.

It is handy to place a sheet of cardstock in between the pages when working inside the book to prevent bleed through or indentation marks to the pages behind. All the pages are also single sided so that you can remove them from the book for easy coloring or framing.

Author: Copyright © 2018 by Iza Bella Creative Art Therapy Studio & Co.
Publisher: AMOBISS, info: izabella.creativeart@gmail.com
Facebook: Iza Bella Creative Art

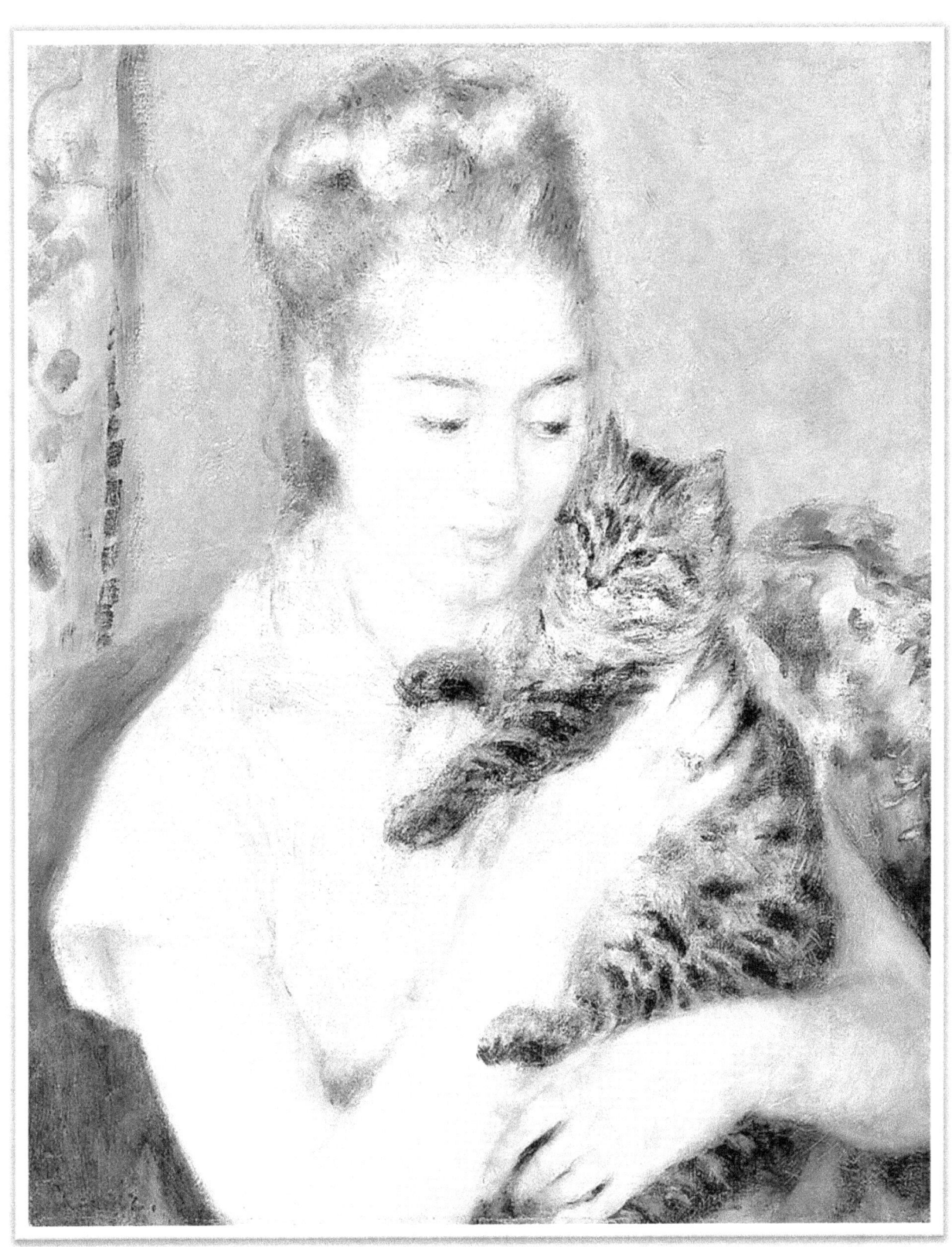

1. Pierre-Auguste Renoir (1841-1919), Woman with a Cat

2. Vincent van Gogh (1853-1890), Summer: Farmhouse in Provence

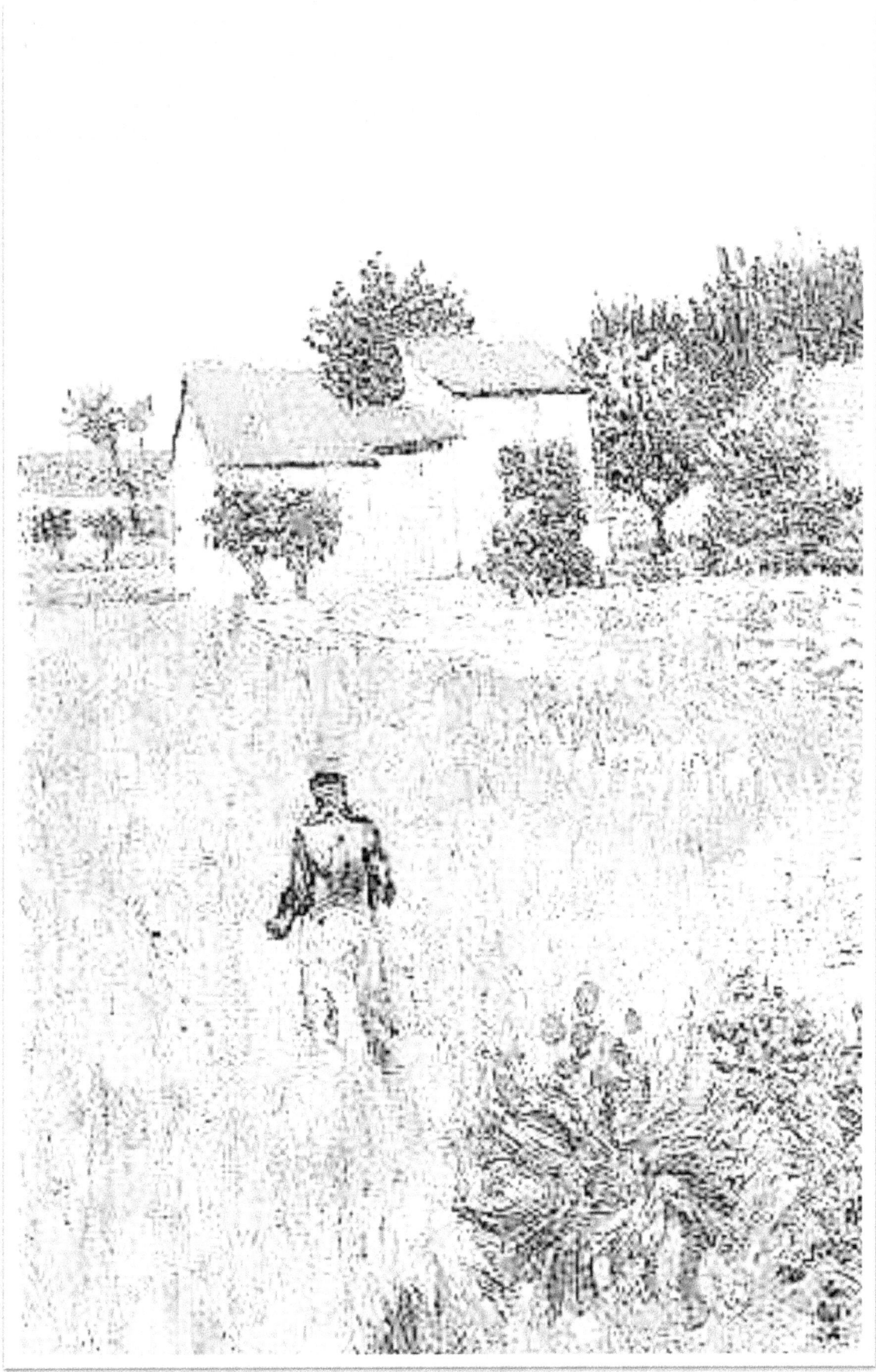

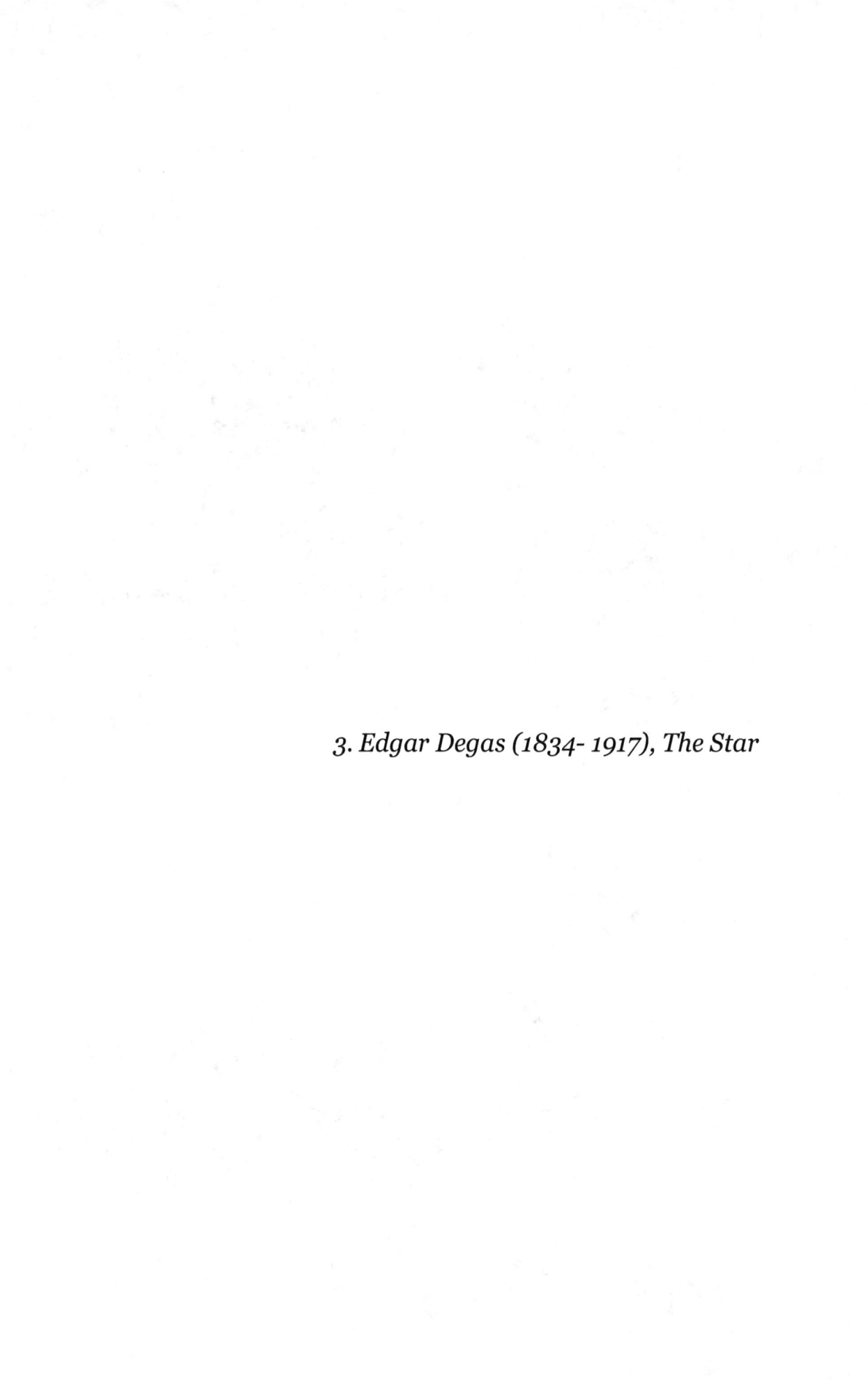

3. Edgar Degas (1834- 1917), The Star

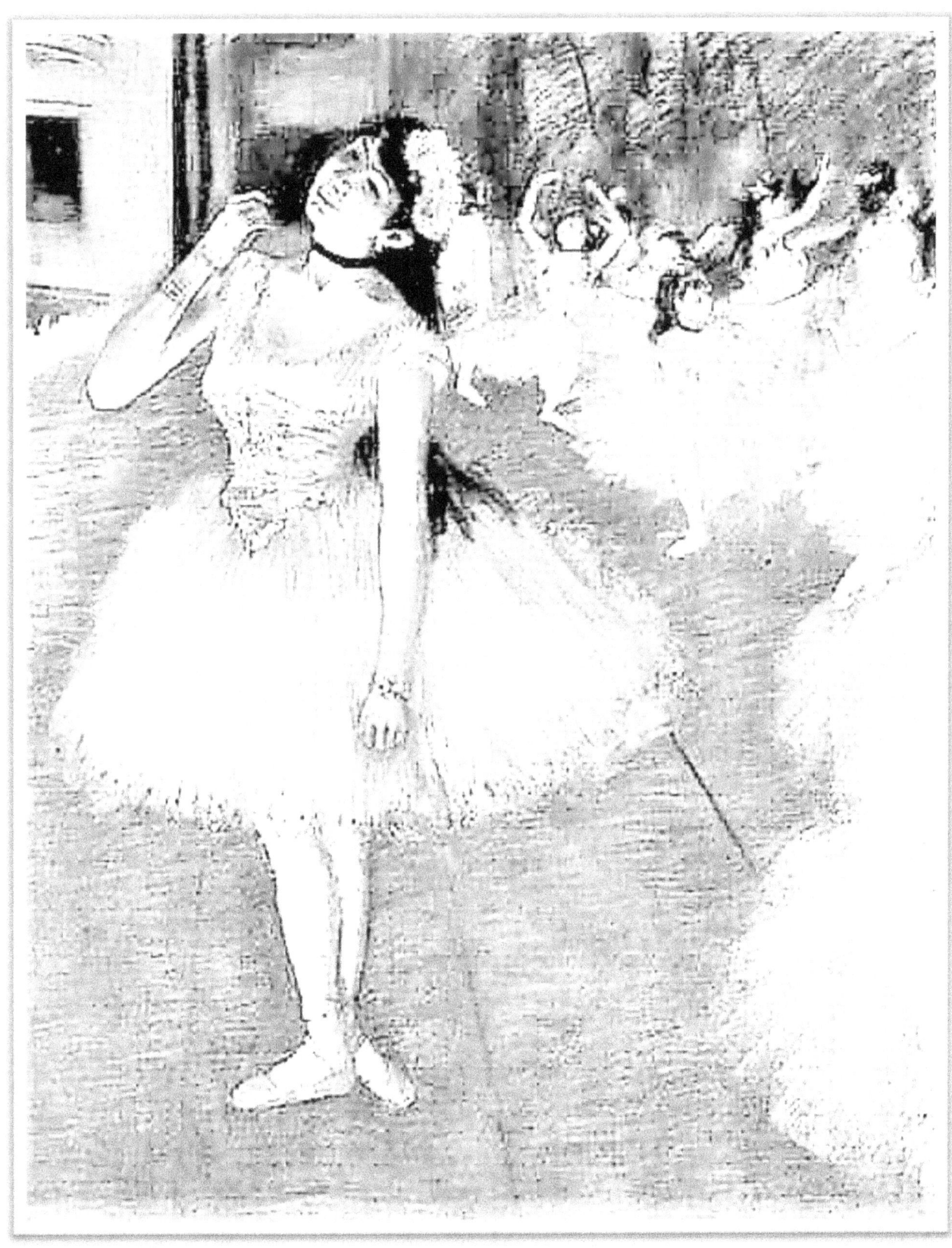

4. van Gogh, Still Life: Vase with Oleanders and Books

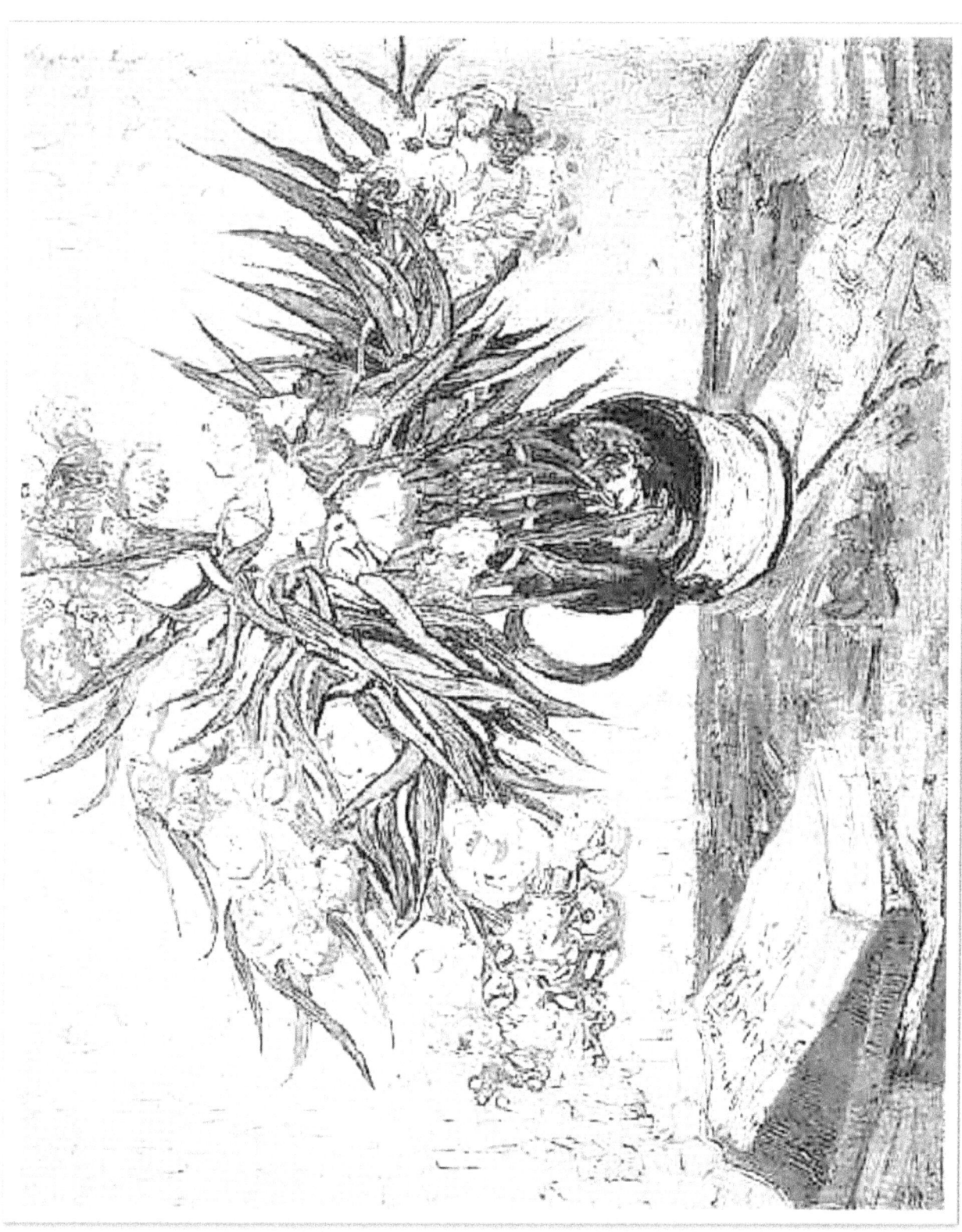

5. Ellen Mary Cassatt (1844-1926), The Pink Sash

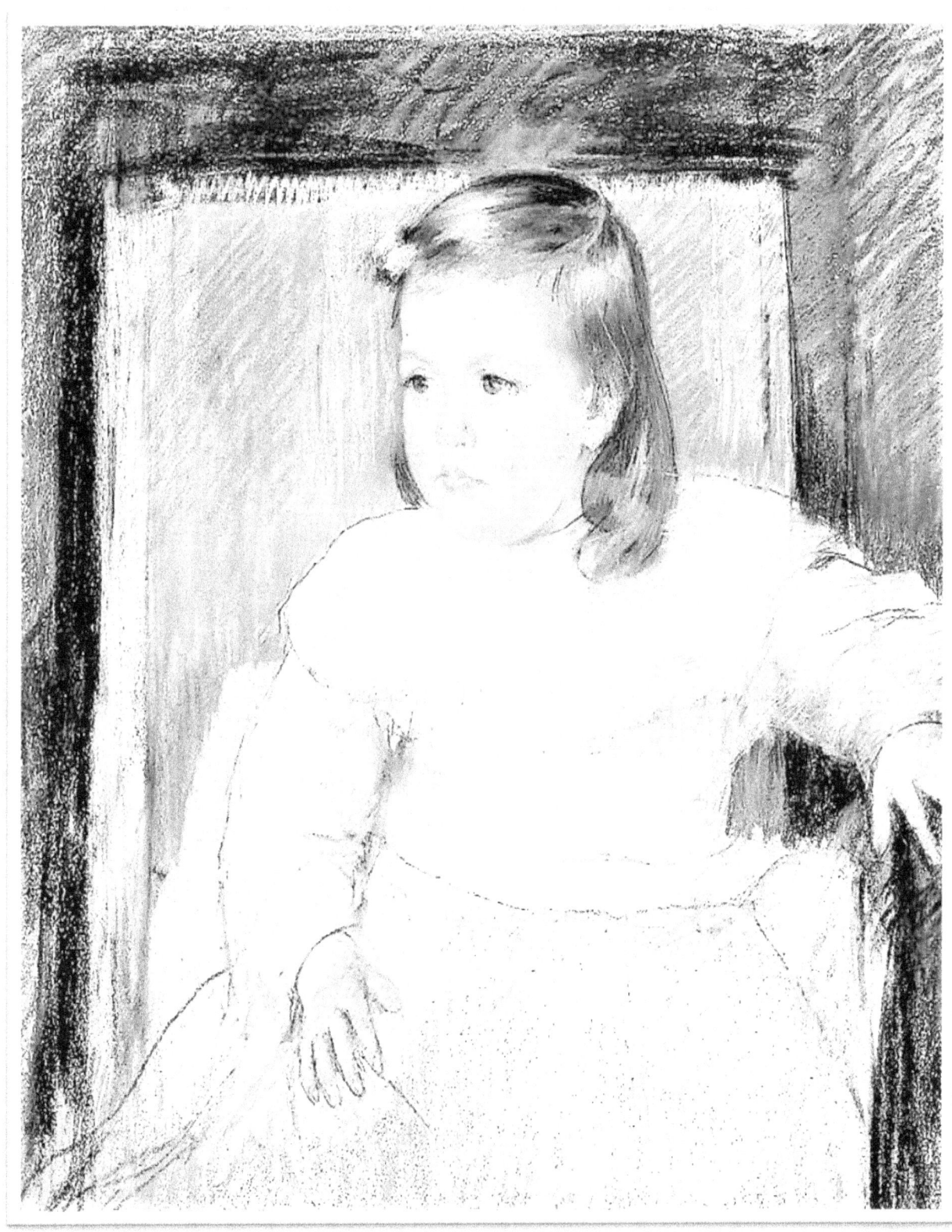

6. Claude Monet (1840-1926), Three Poplar Trees in the Autumn

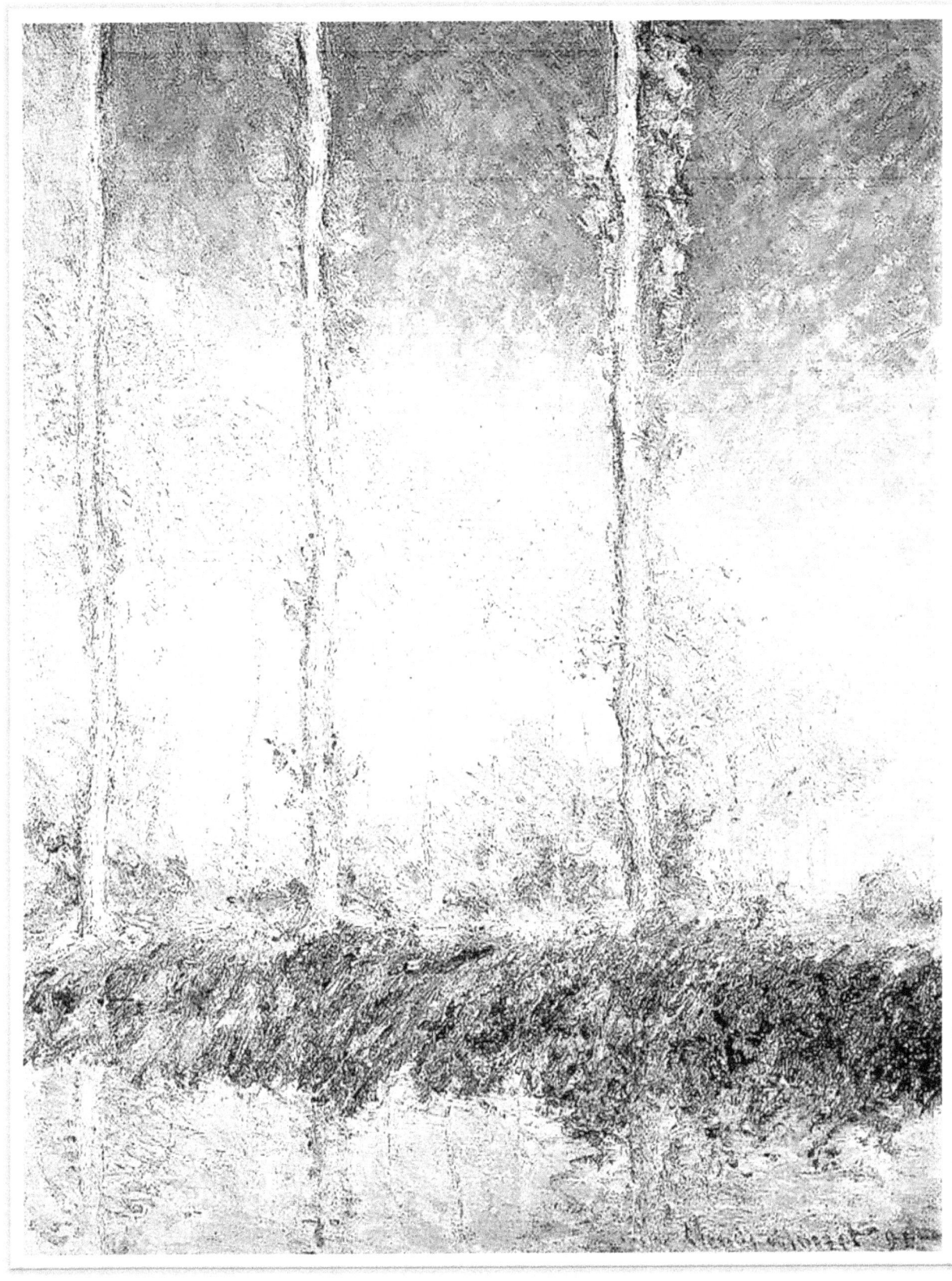

7. van Gogh, Two Diggers Among Trees

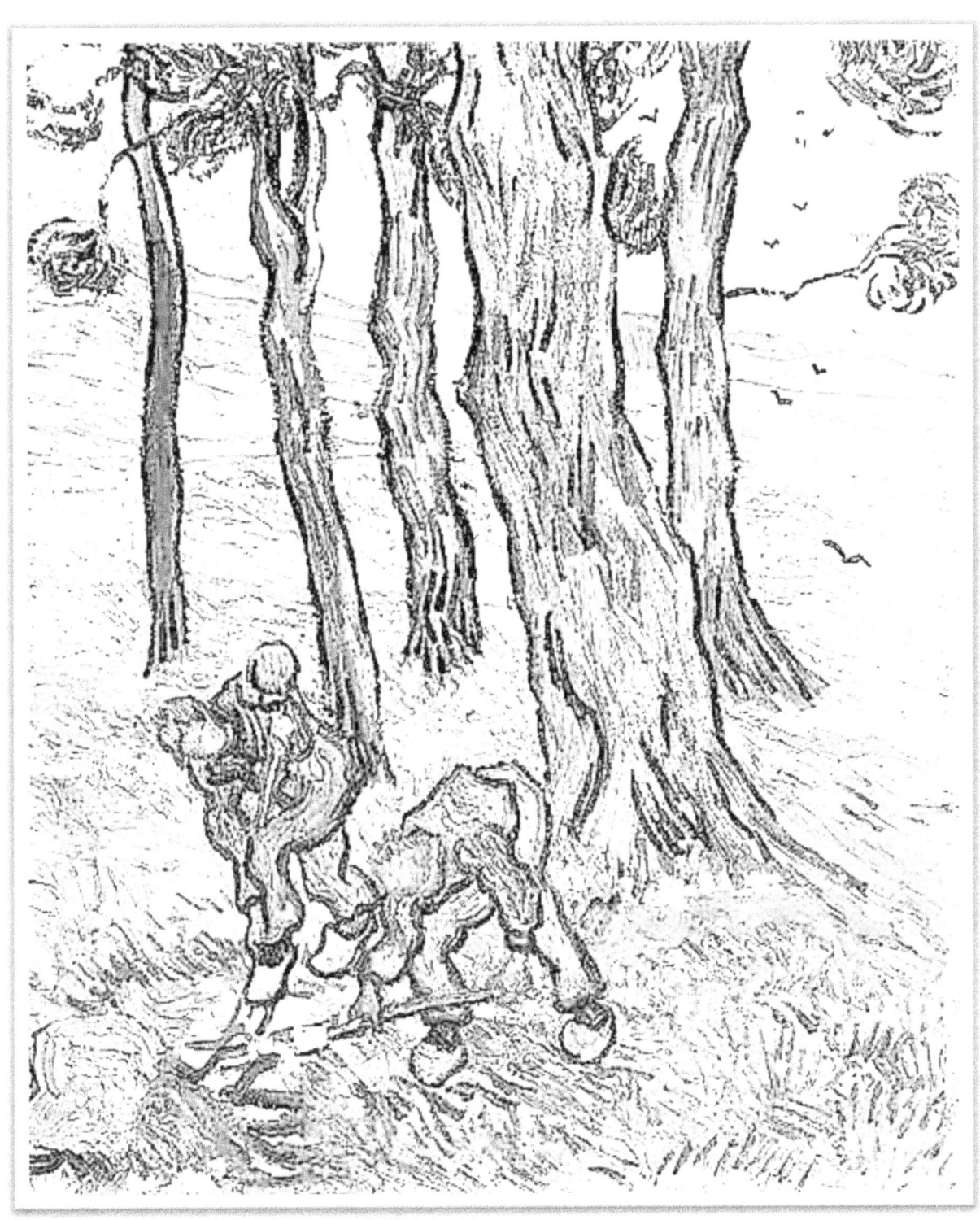

8. Cassatt, Young Woman with Auburn Hair in a Pink Blouse

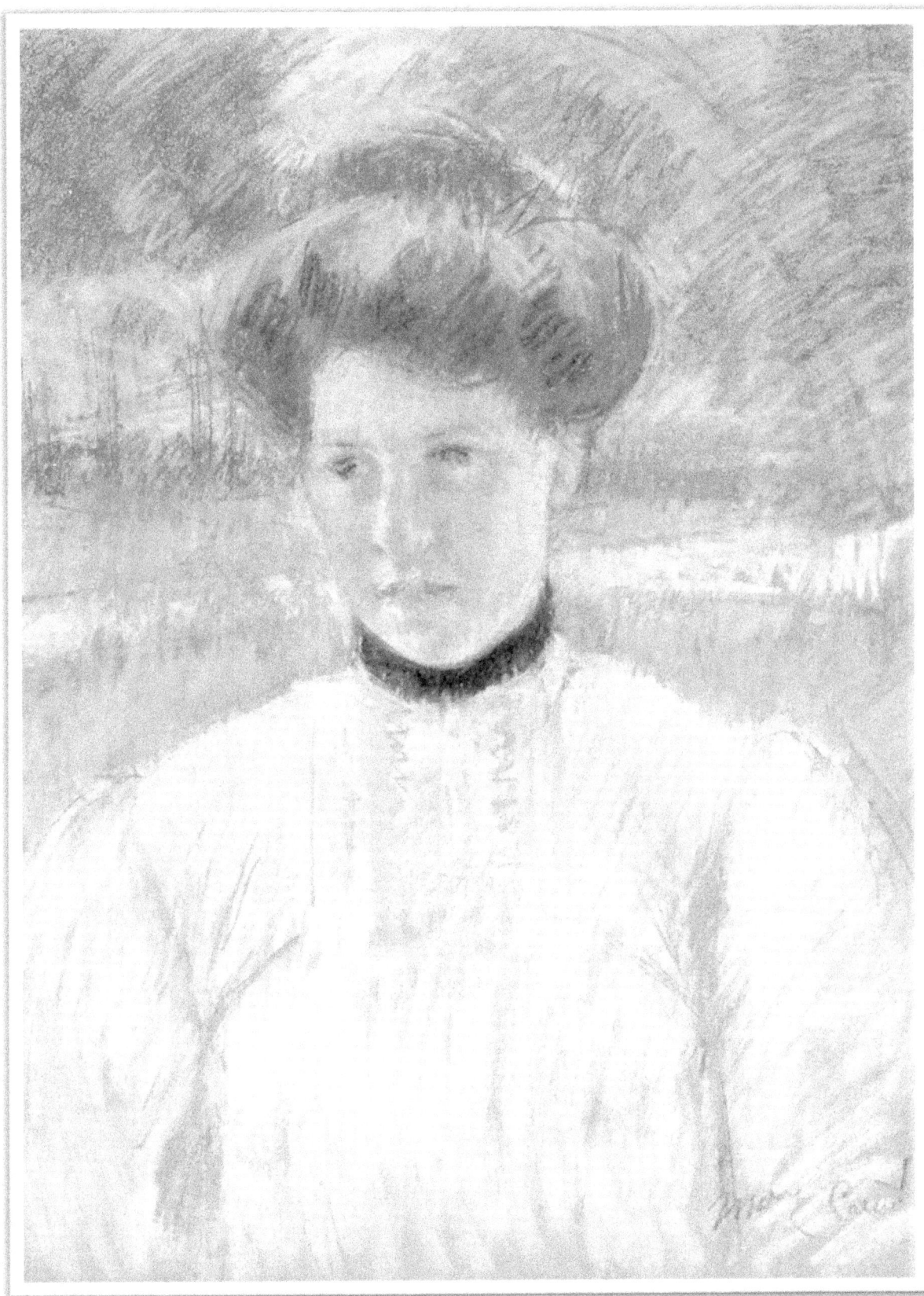

9. *Renoir, Le Montagne Sainte-Victoire*

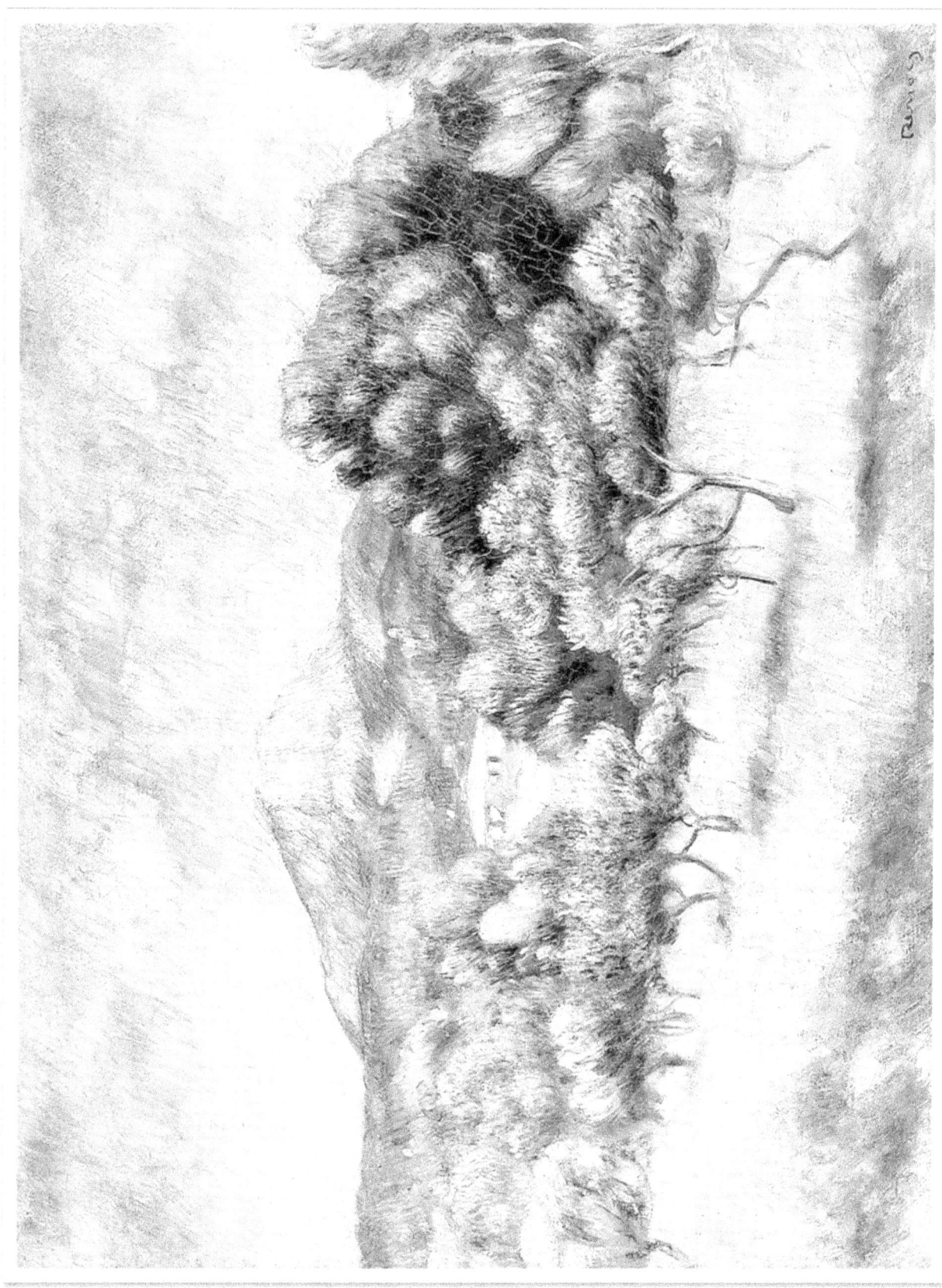

10. *Éduard Manet (1832-1883), The Rest, Portrait of Berthe Morisot*

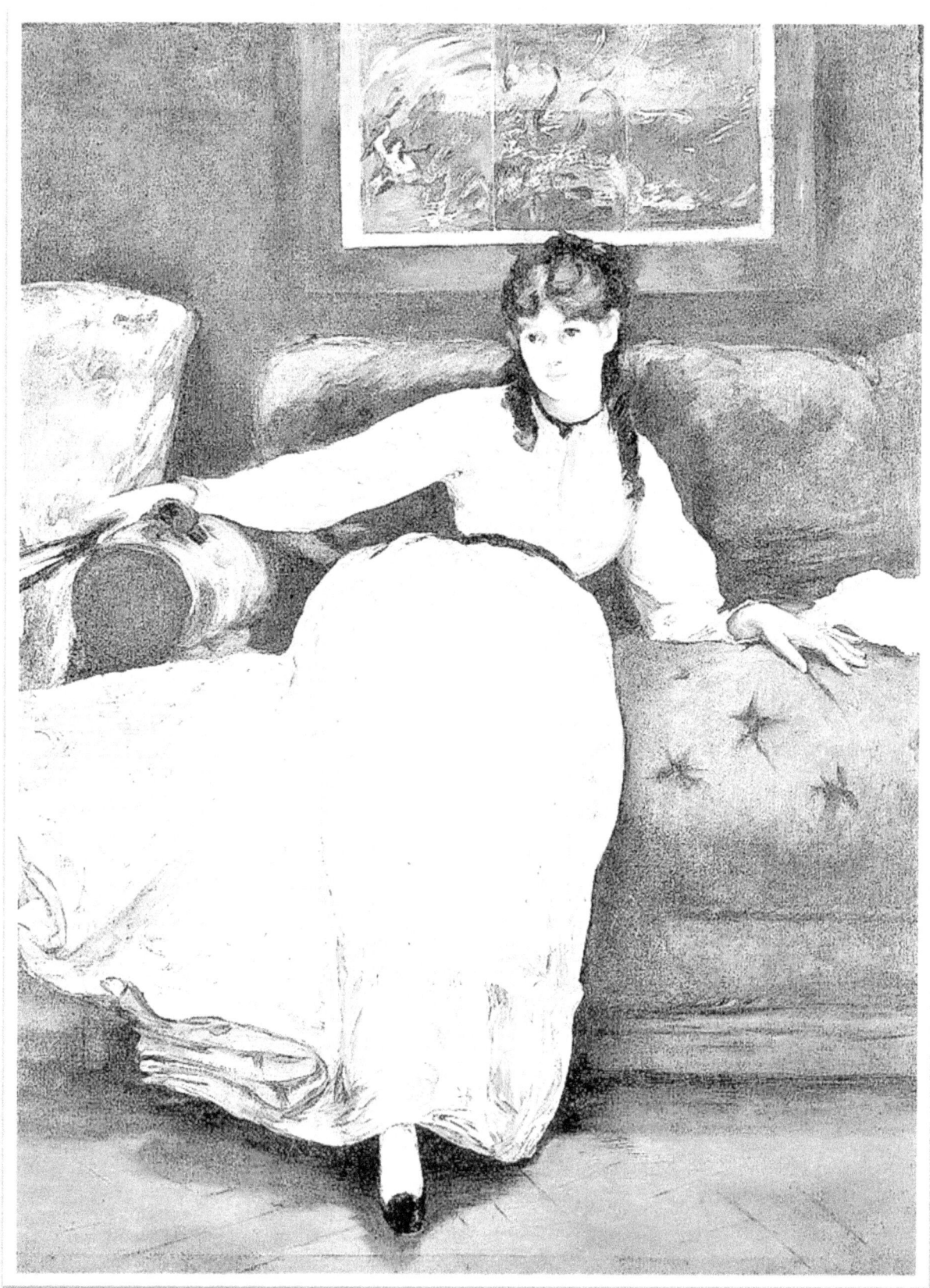

11. van Gogh, Two Poplars on a Road Through the Hills

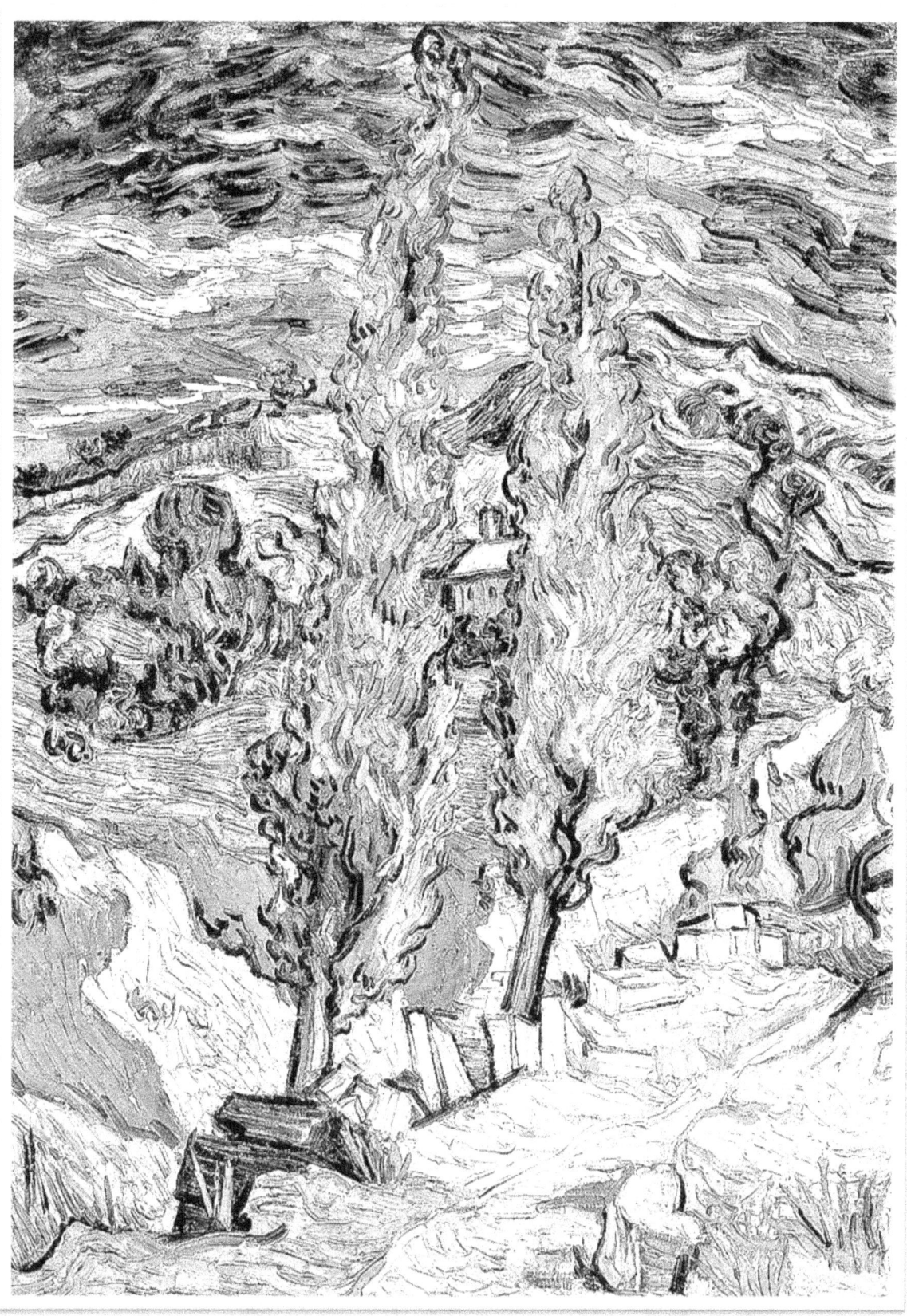

12. Renoir, La Promenade

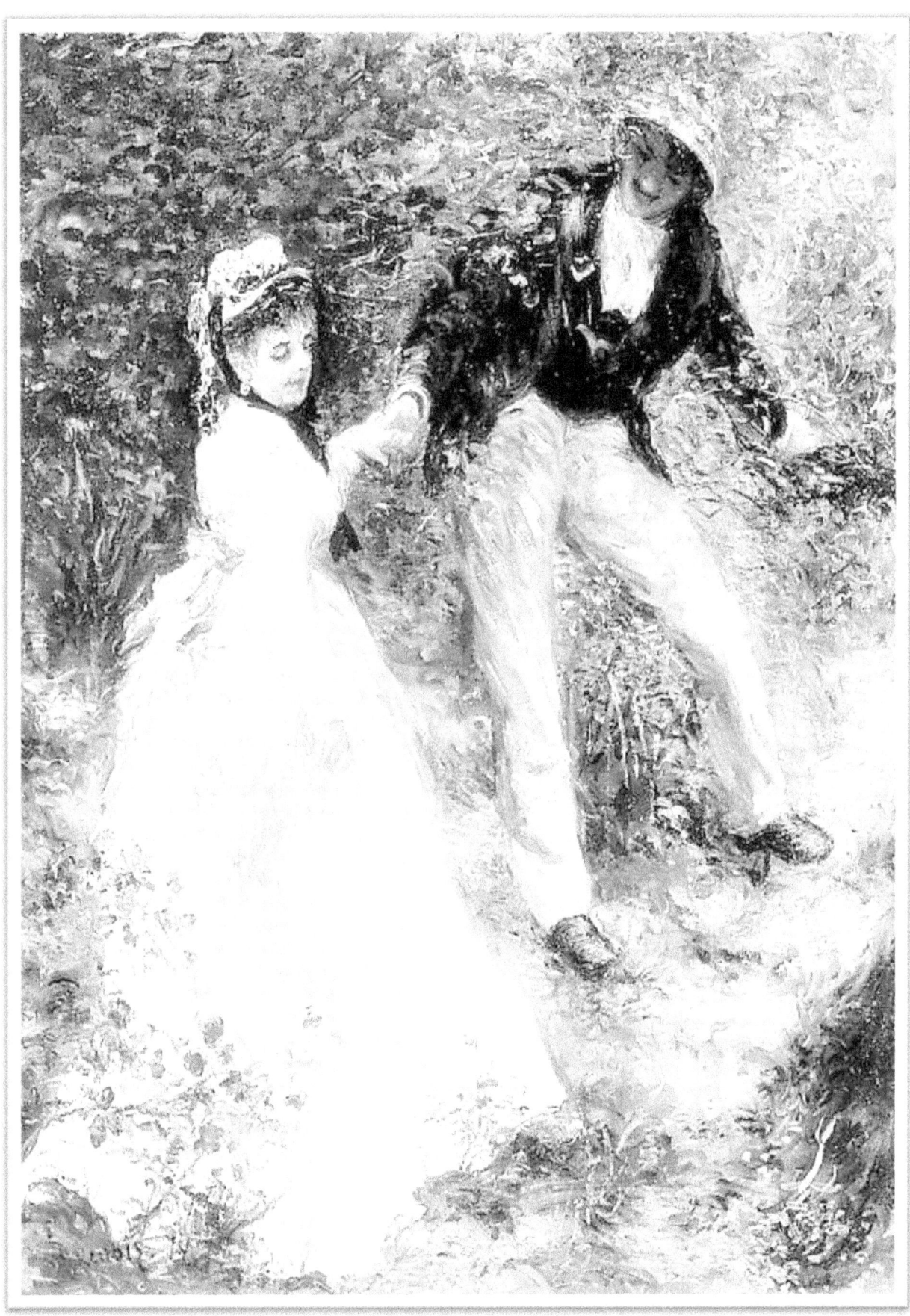

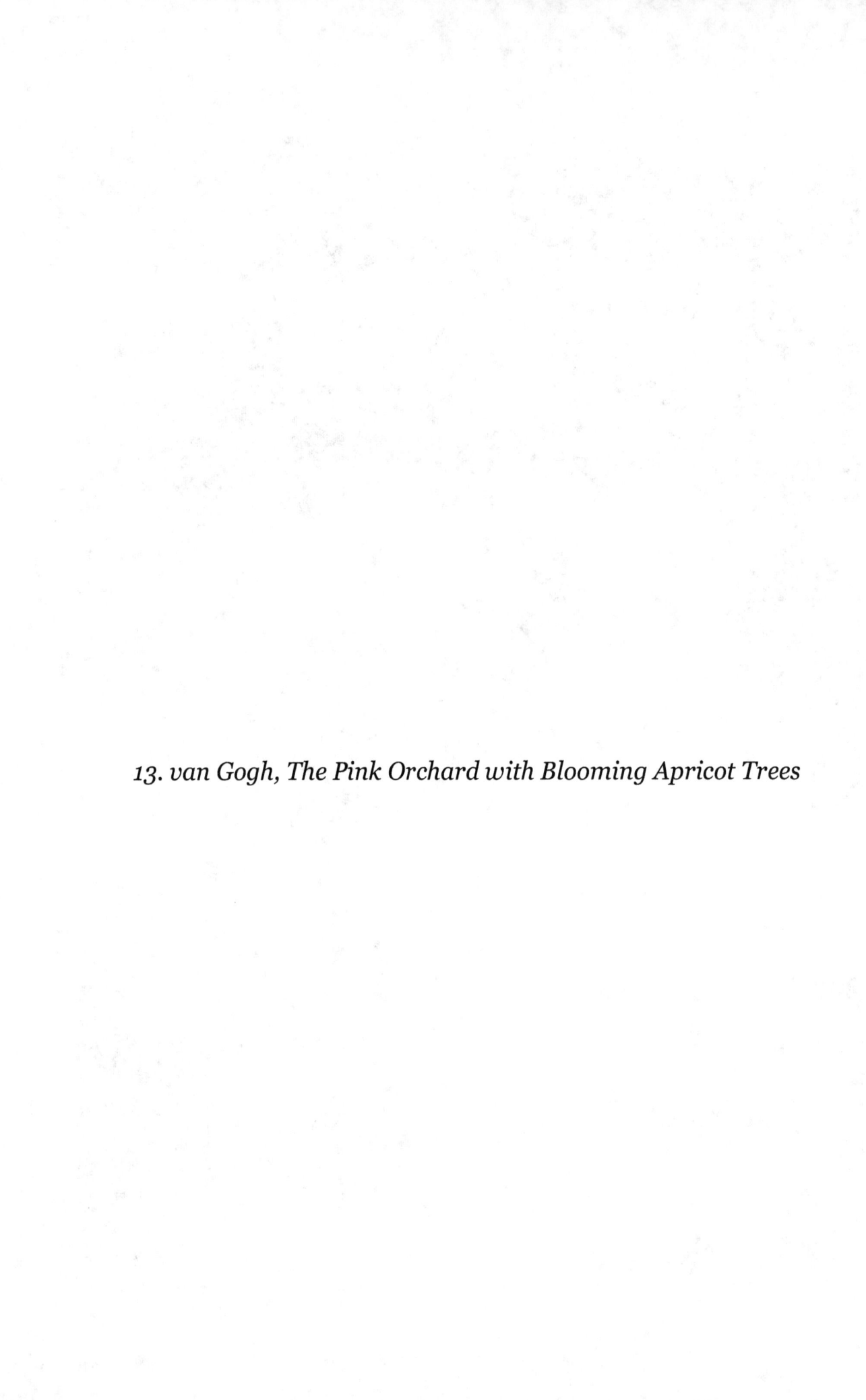

13. van Gogh, The Pink Orchard with Blooming Apricot Trees

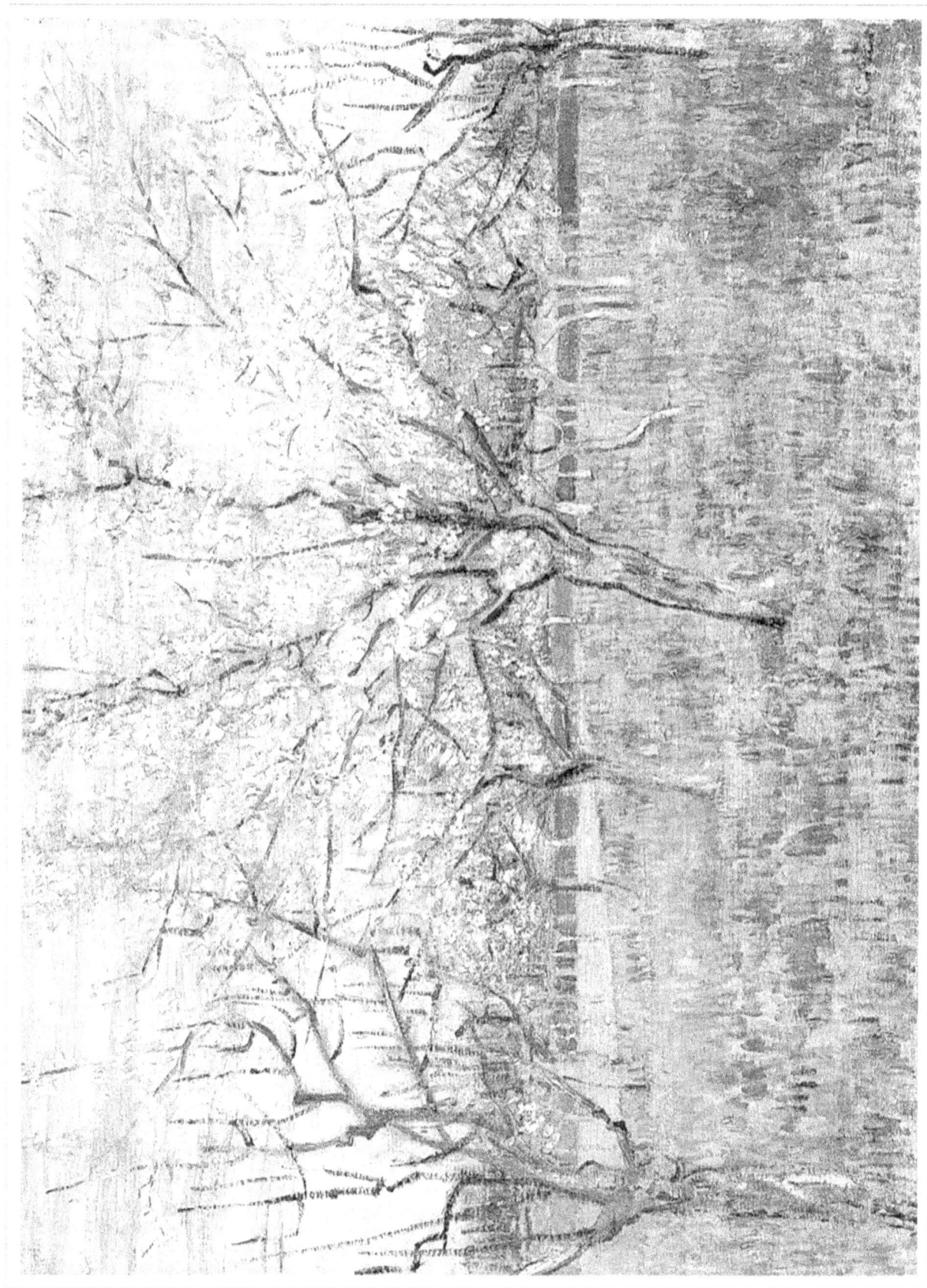

14. Henri de Toulouse-Lautrec (1864-1901), *Jane Avril*

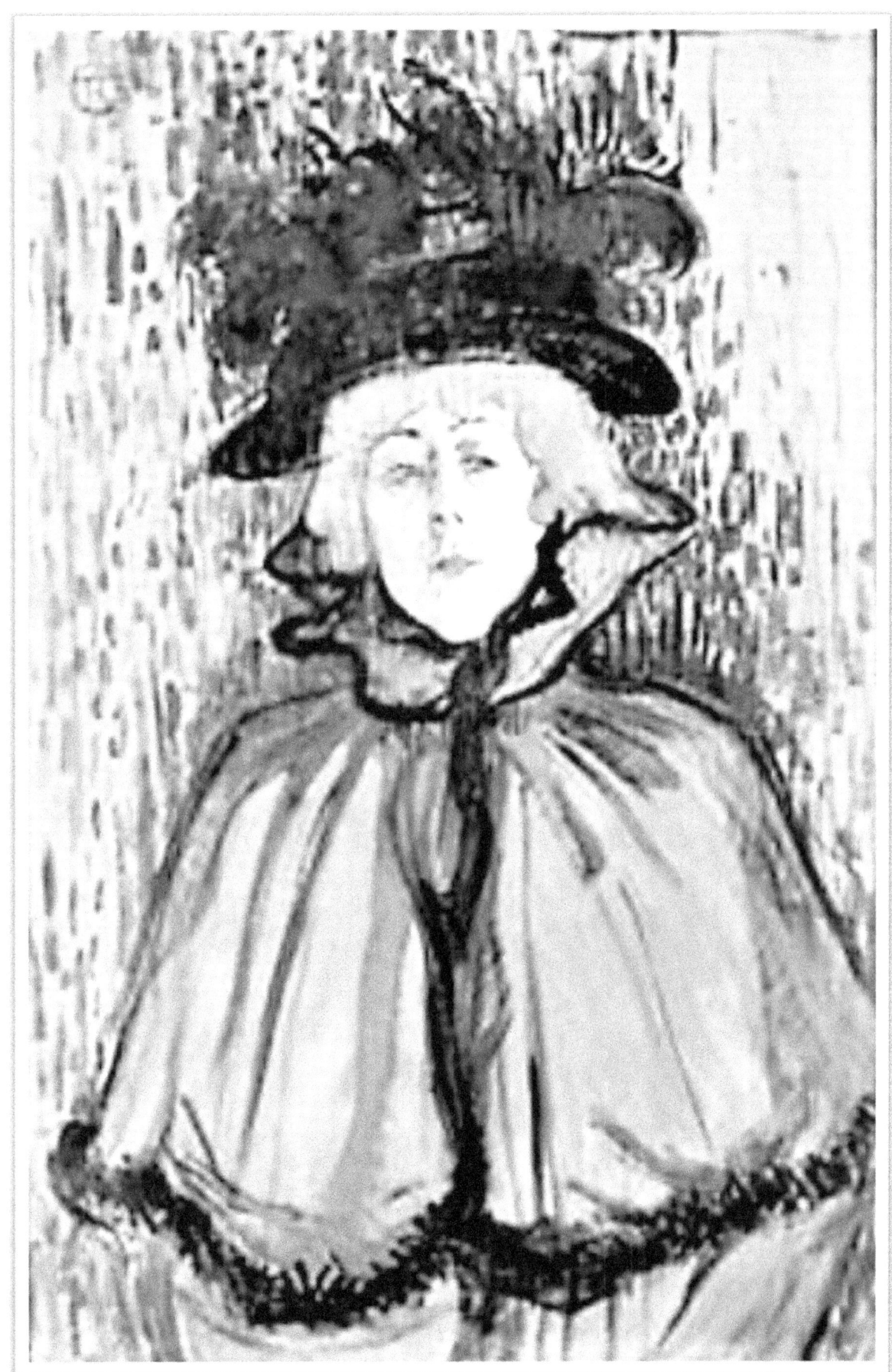

15. Renoir, The Luncheon of the Boating Party

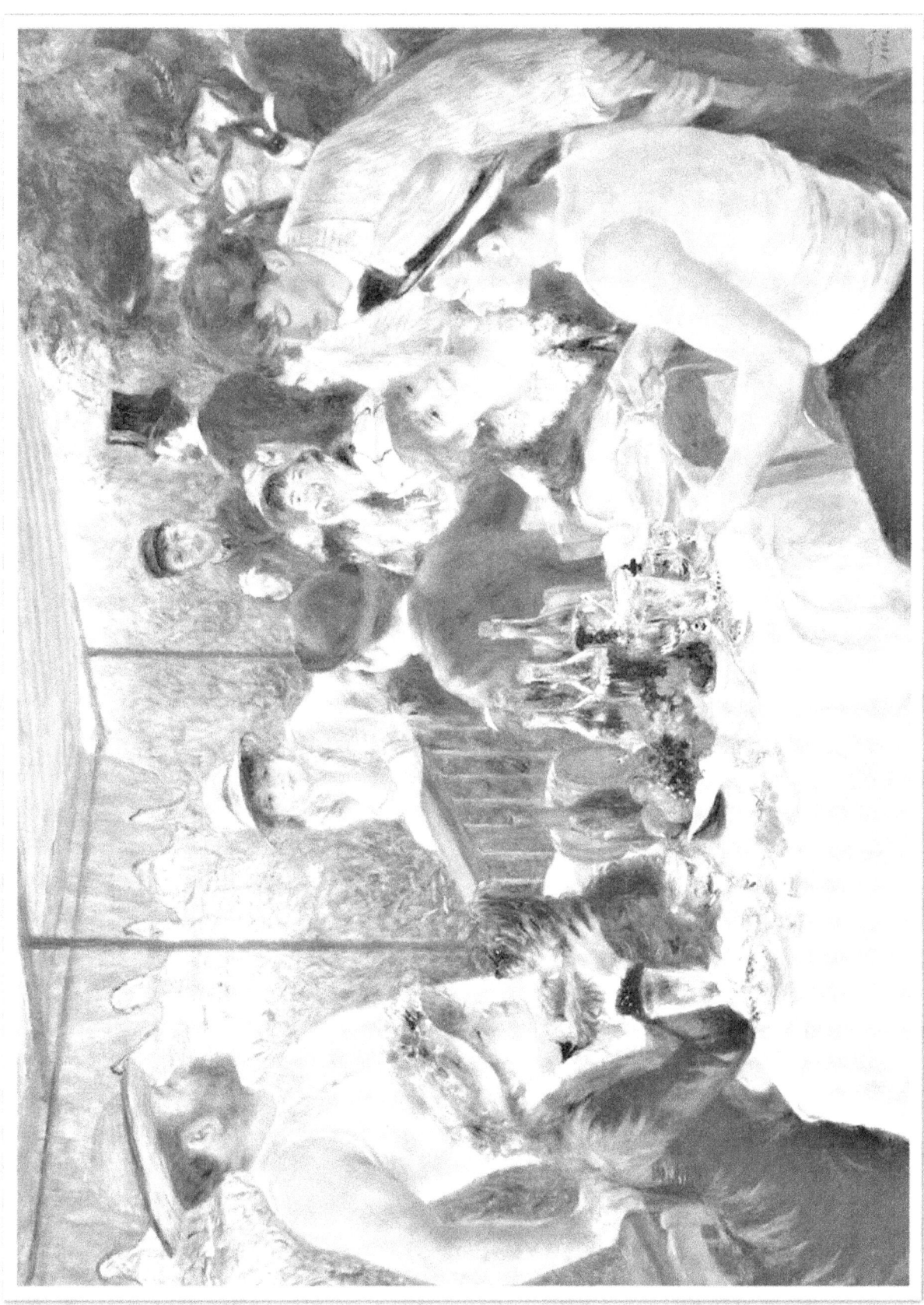

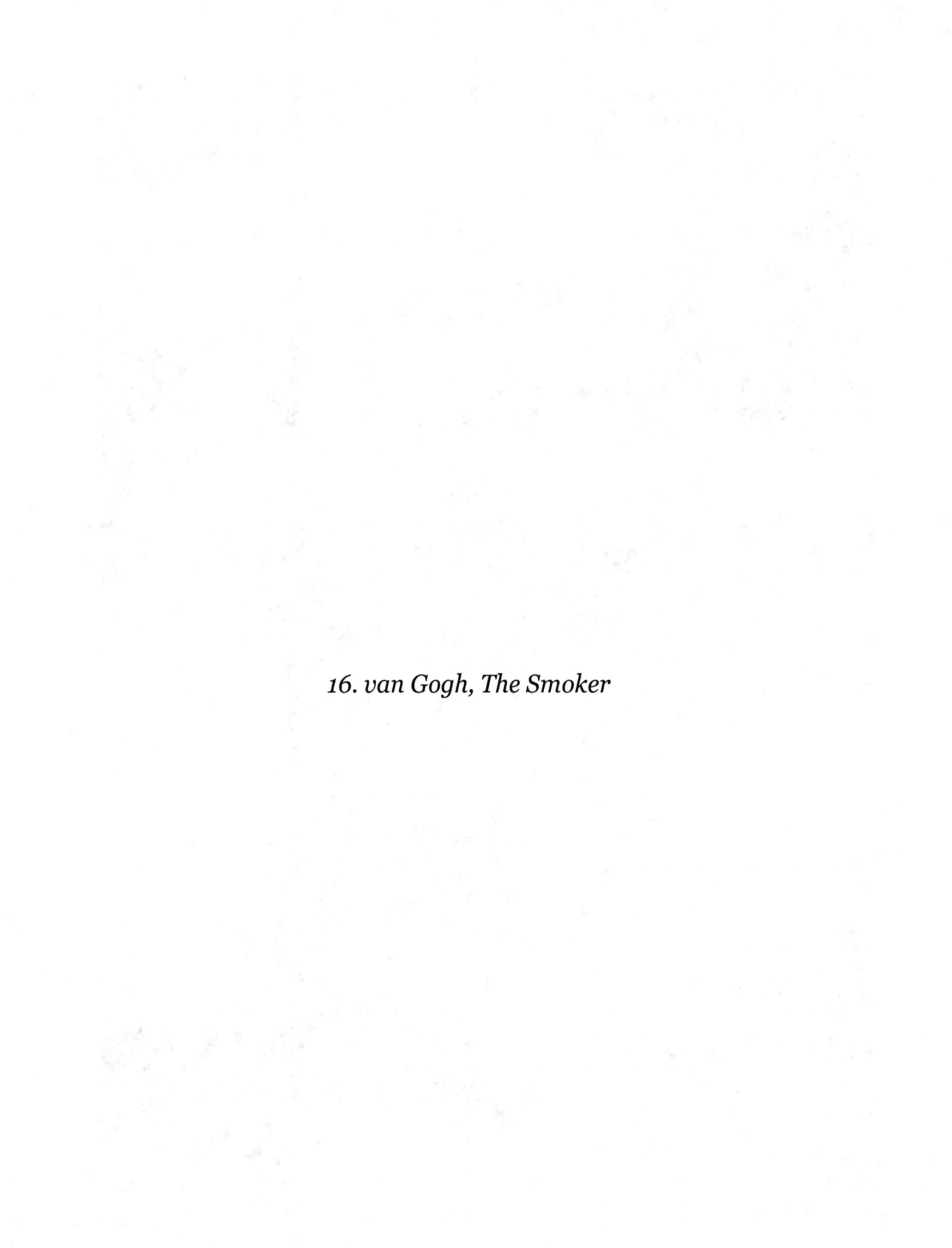

16. van Gogh, The Smoker

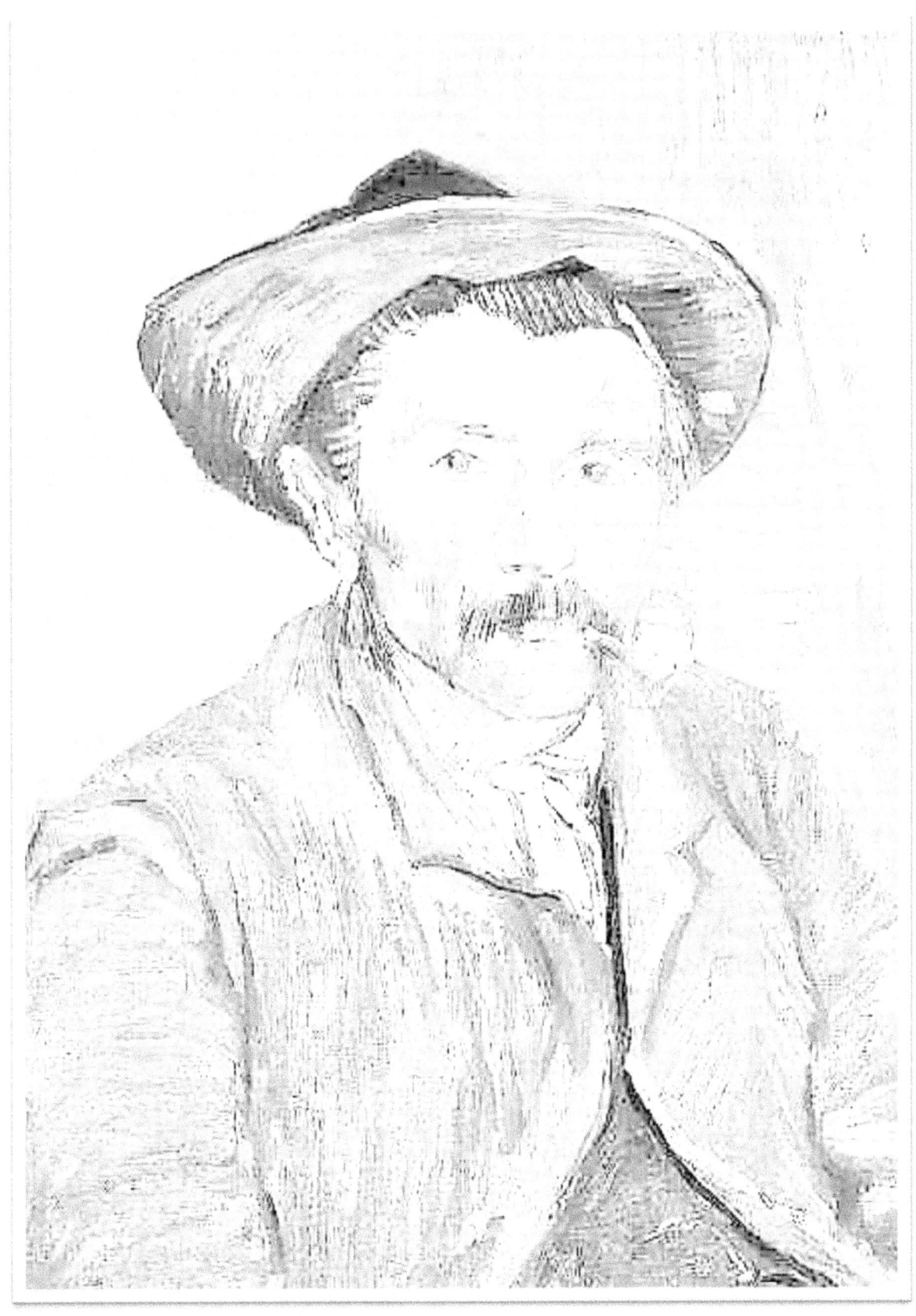

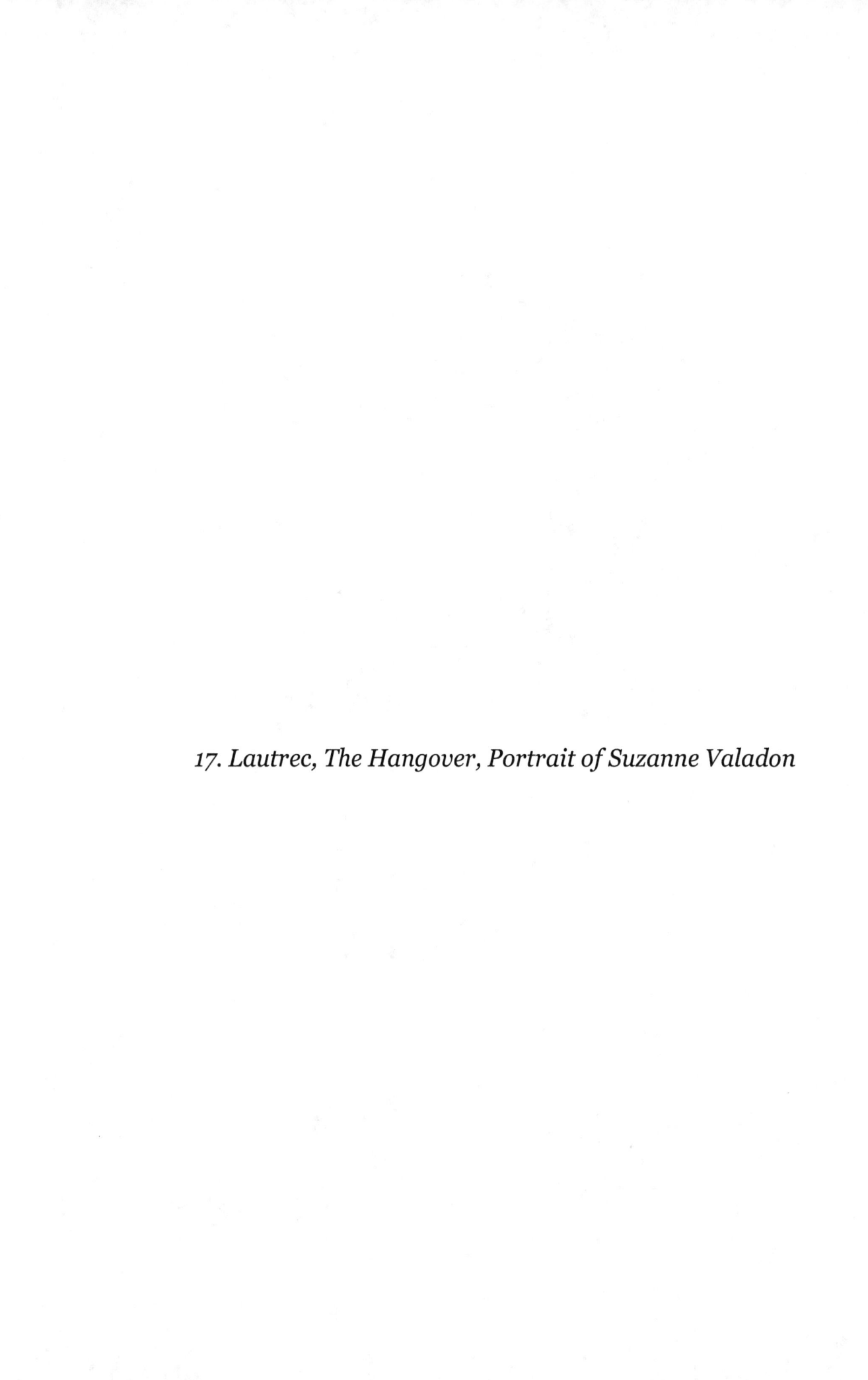

17. Lautrec, The Hangover, Portrait of Suzanne Valadon

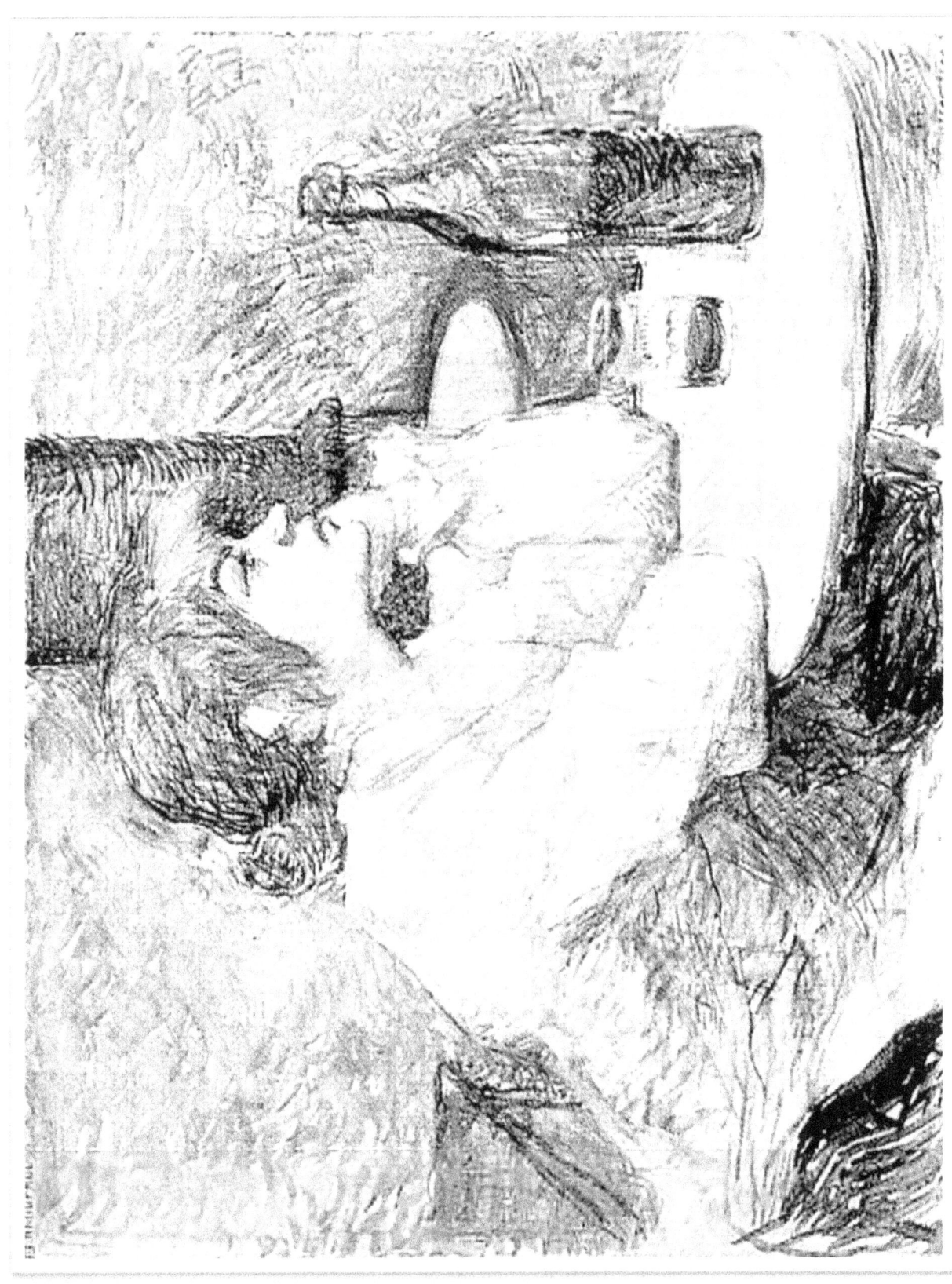

18. Renoir, Dance at Bougival

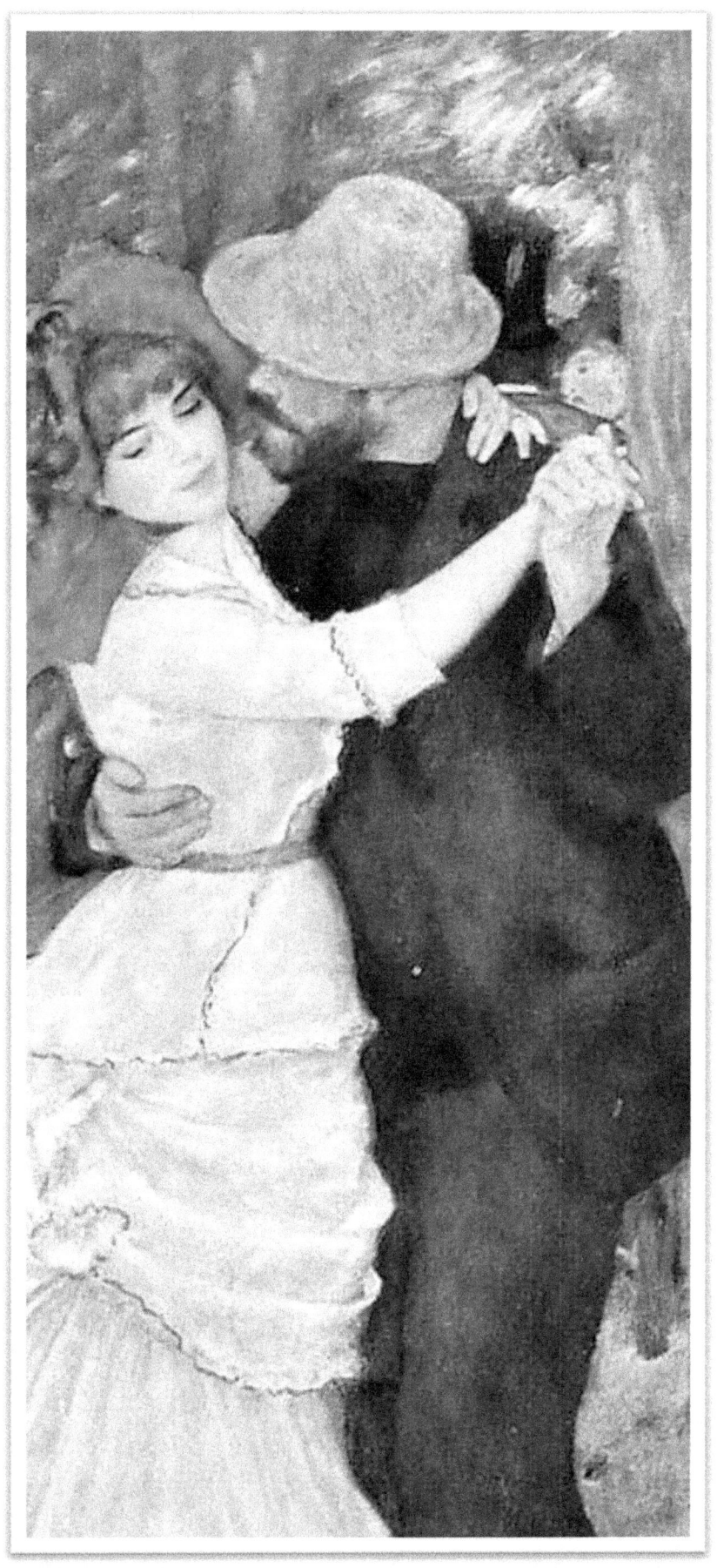

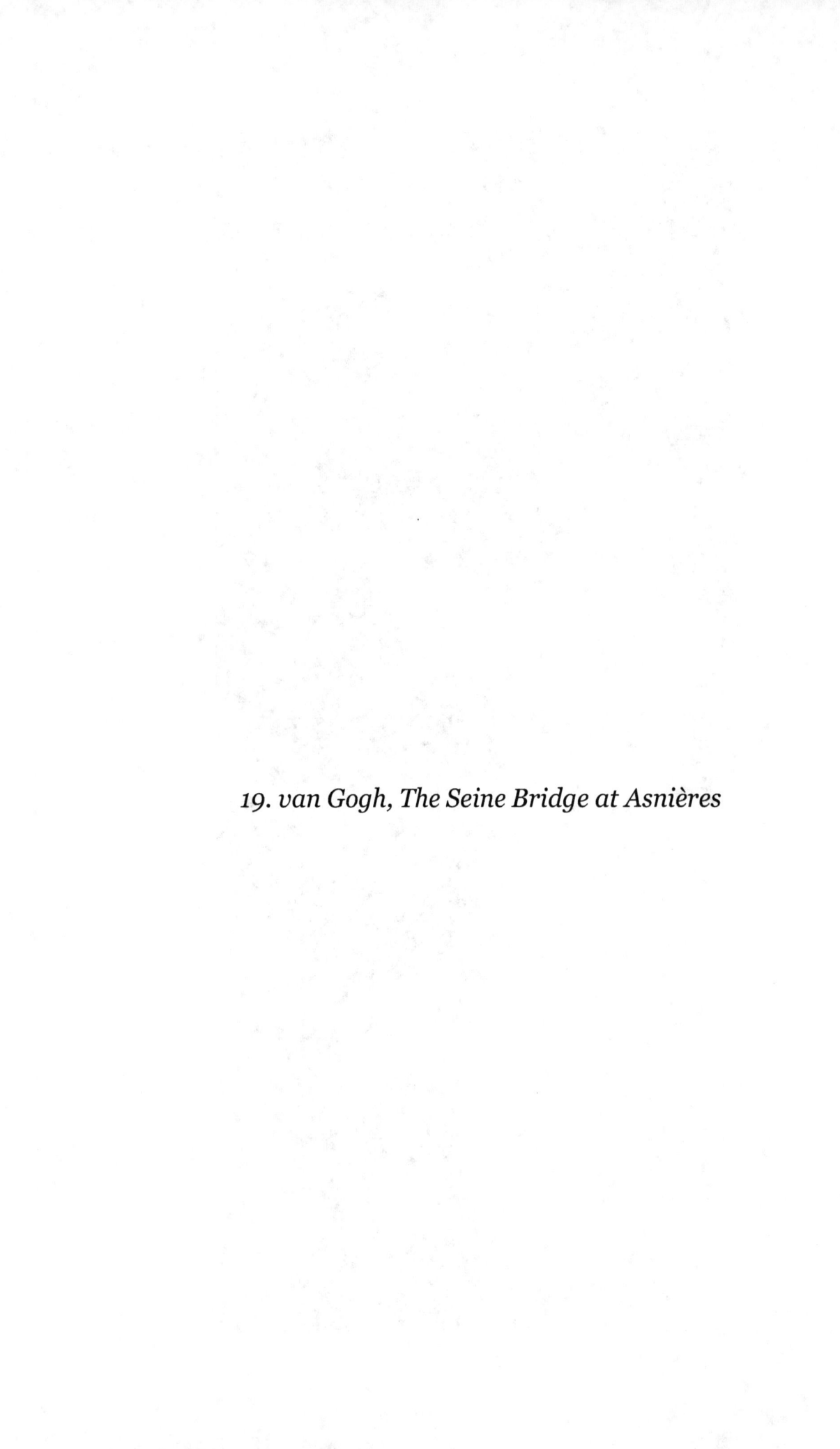

19. van Gogh, *The Seine Bridge at Asnières*

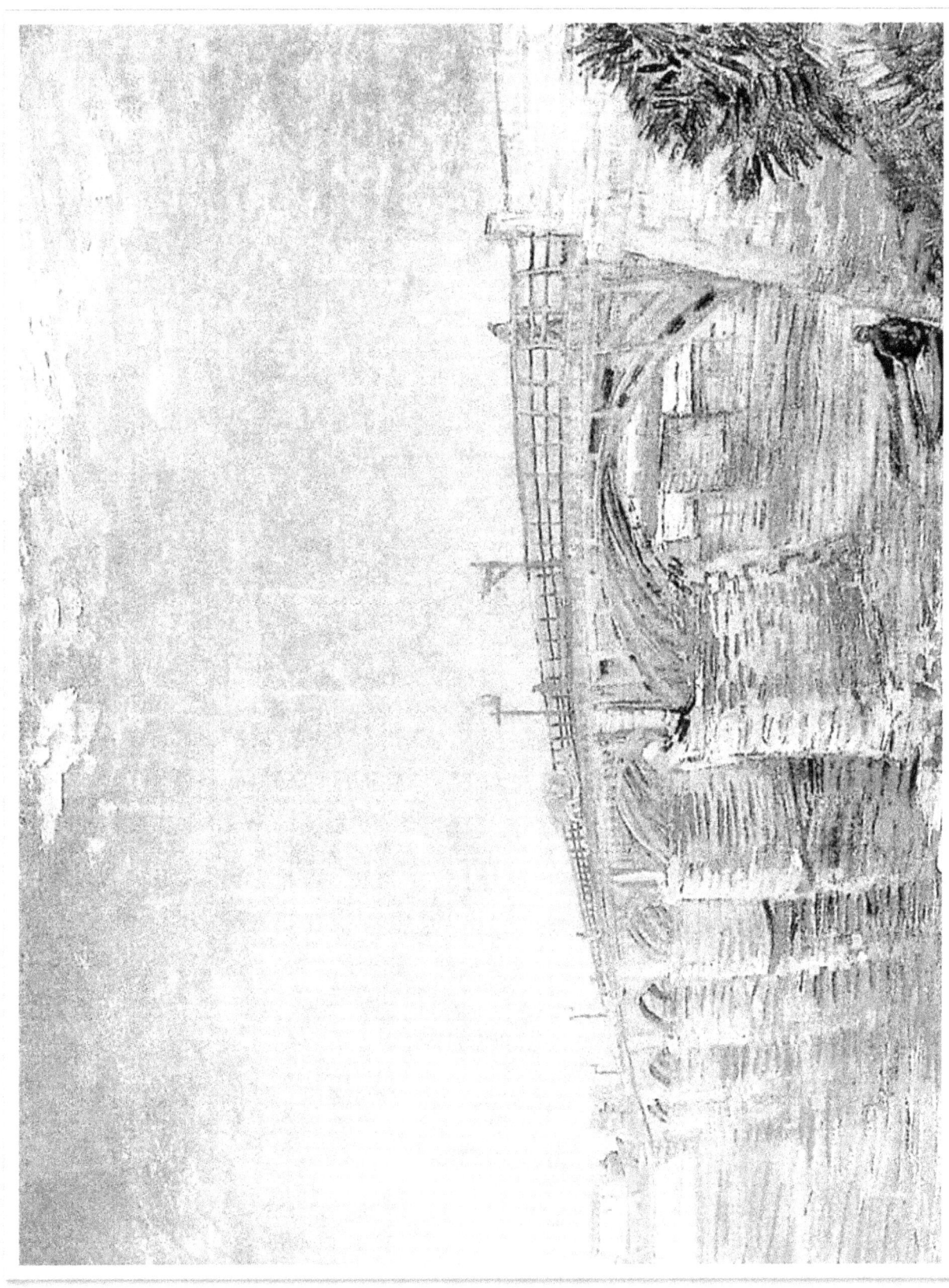

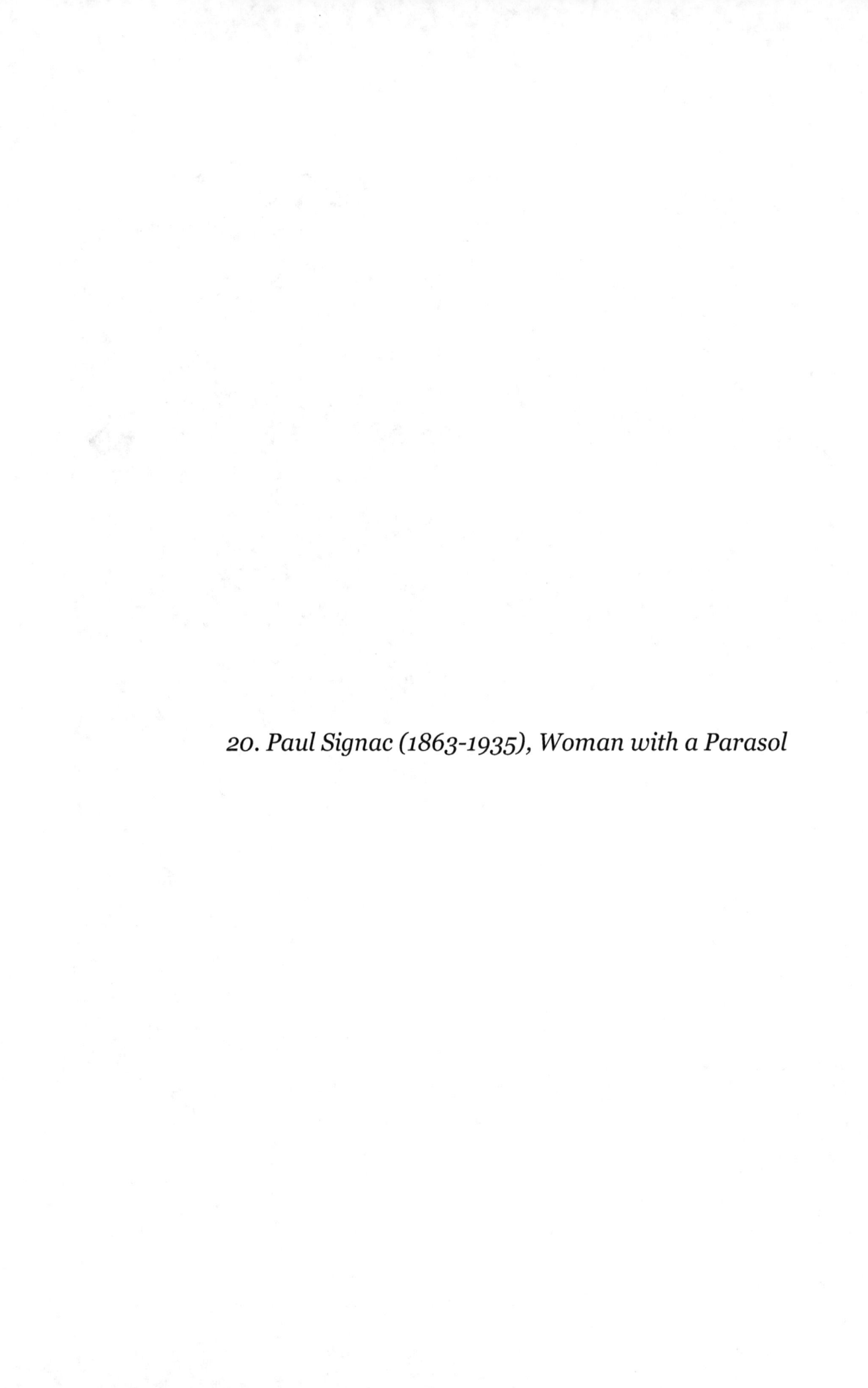

20. Paul Signac (1863-1935), *Woman with a Parasol*

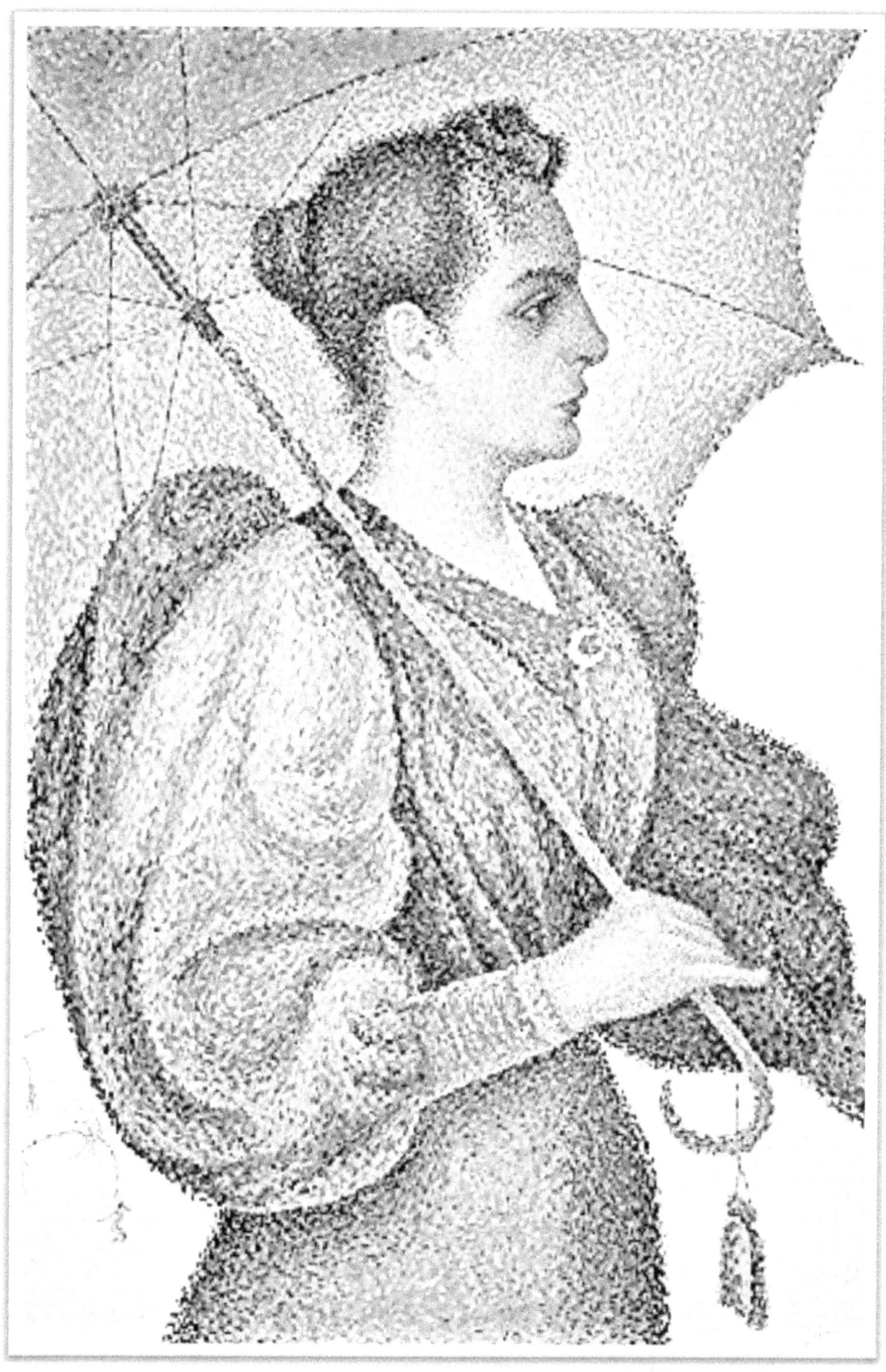

21. Renoir, The Artist's Family

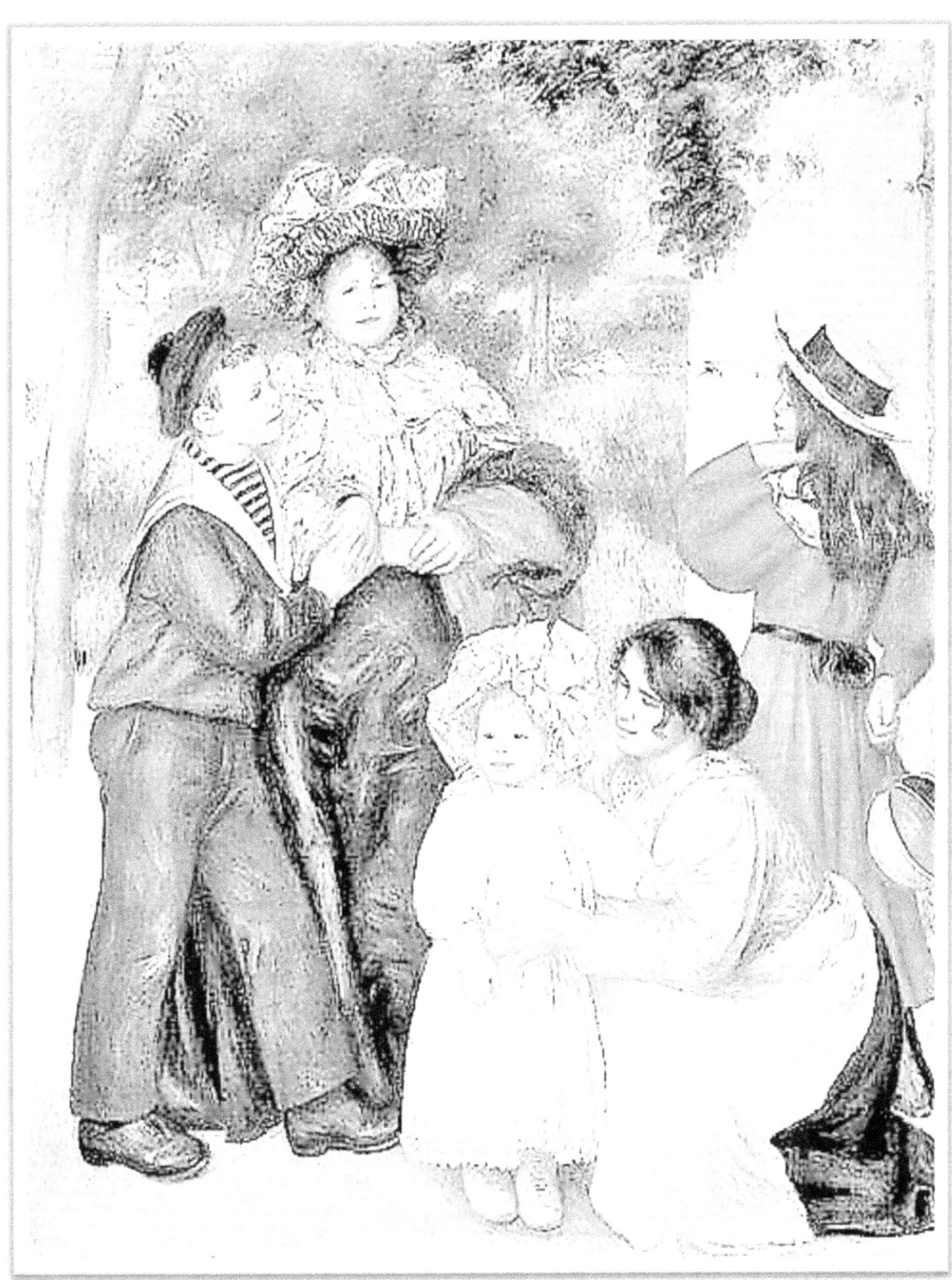

22. Paul Gauguin (1848-1903), Three Tahitian Women

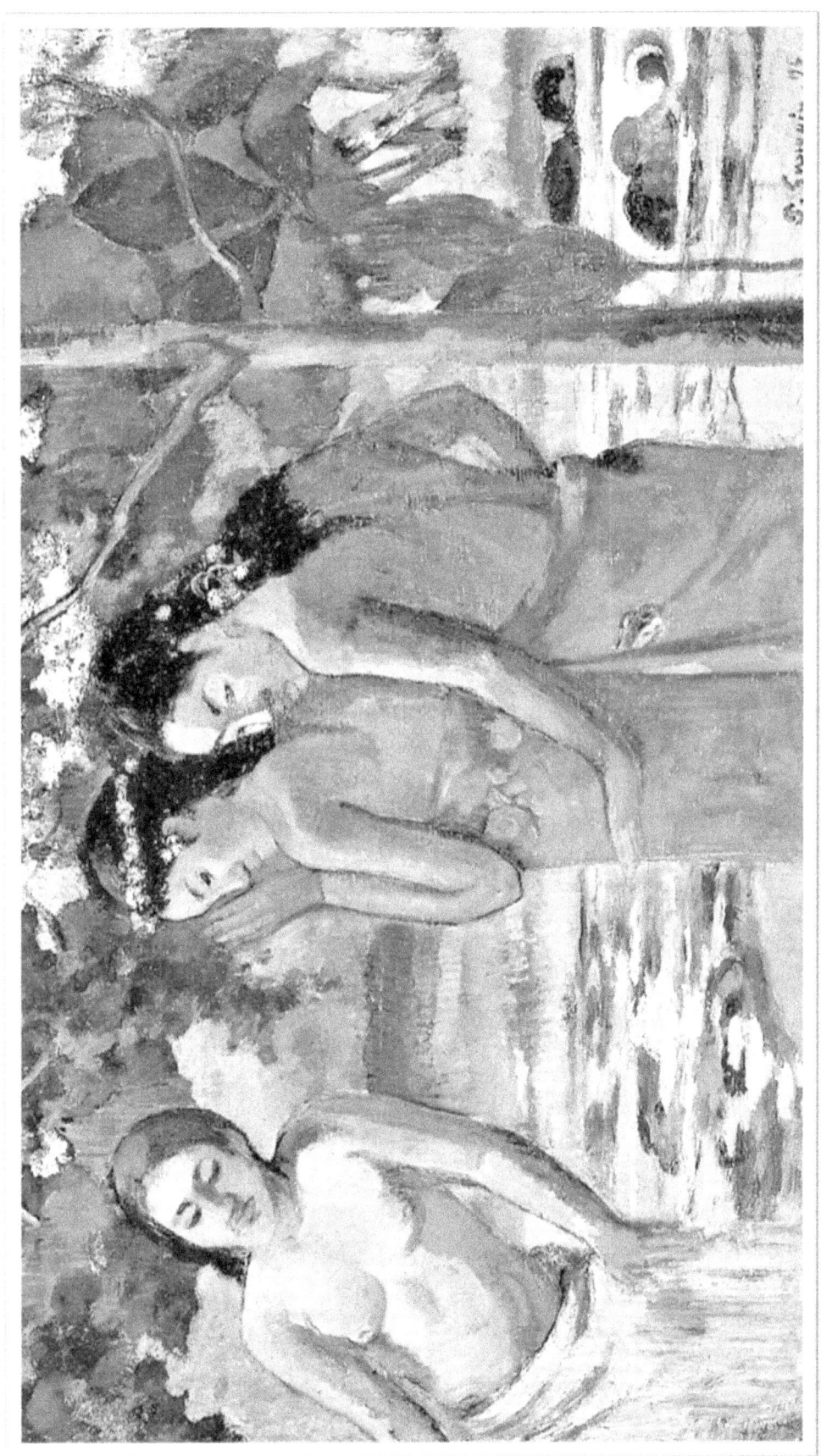

23. *Lautrec, Woman in the Garden of Monsieur Forest*

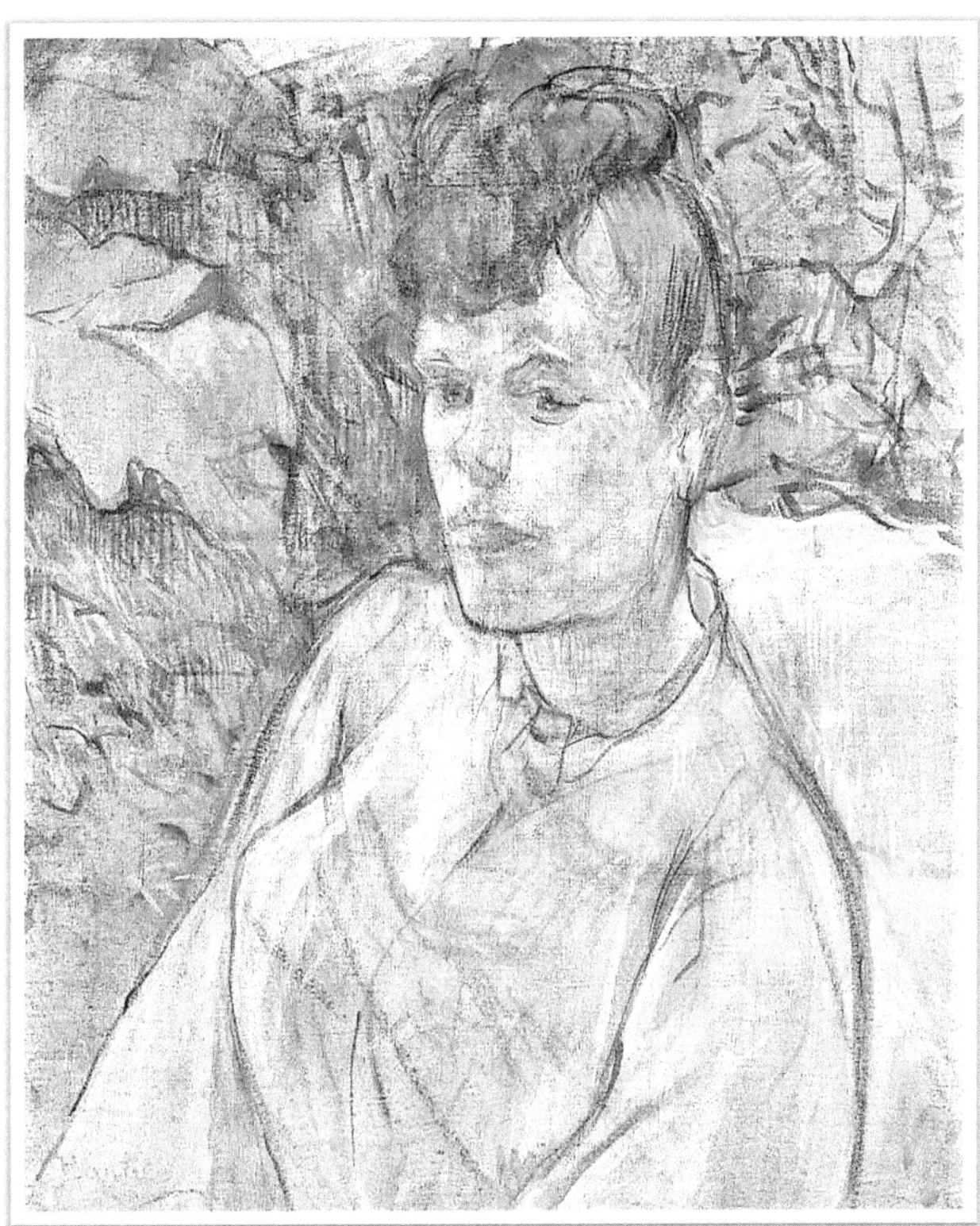

24. Signac, Above Saint-Tropez, The Customs House Pathway

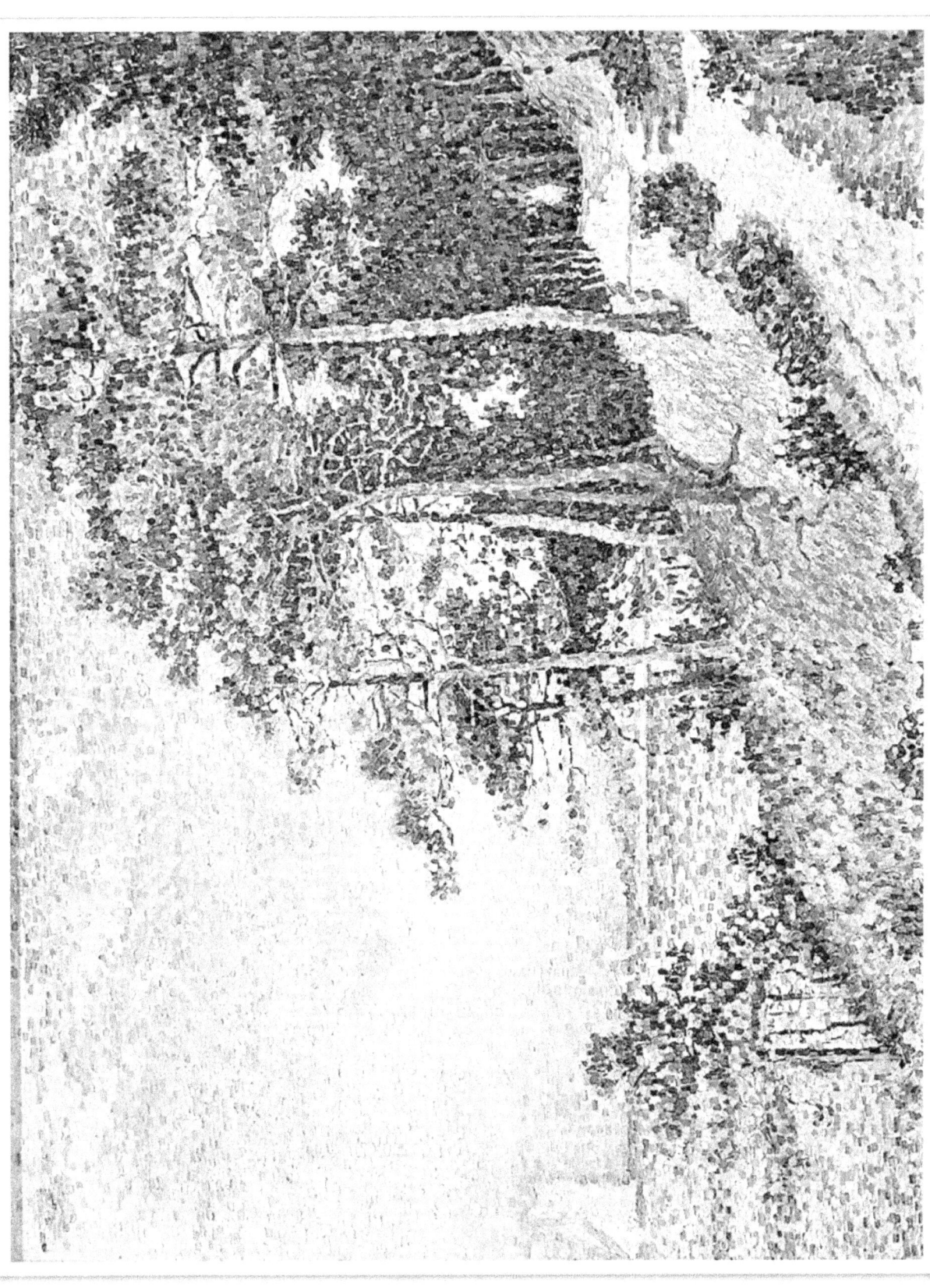

25. *Renoir, Marie Térèse Durand-Ruel Sewing*

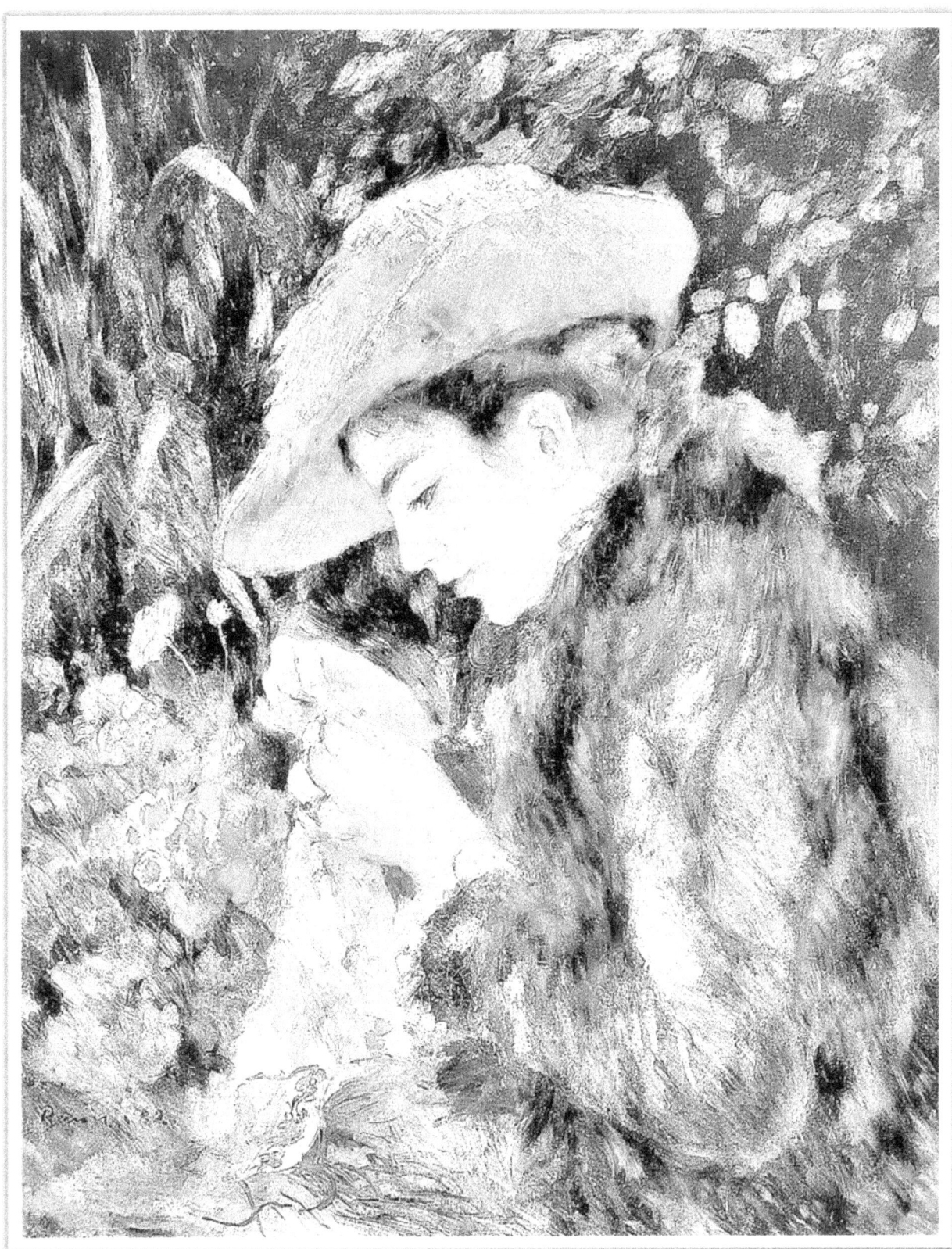

26. Gauguin, Tehamana Has Many Parents, The Ancestors of Tehamana

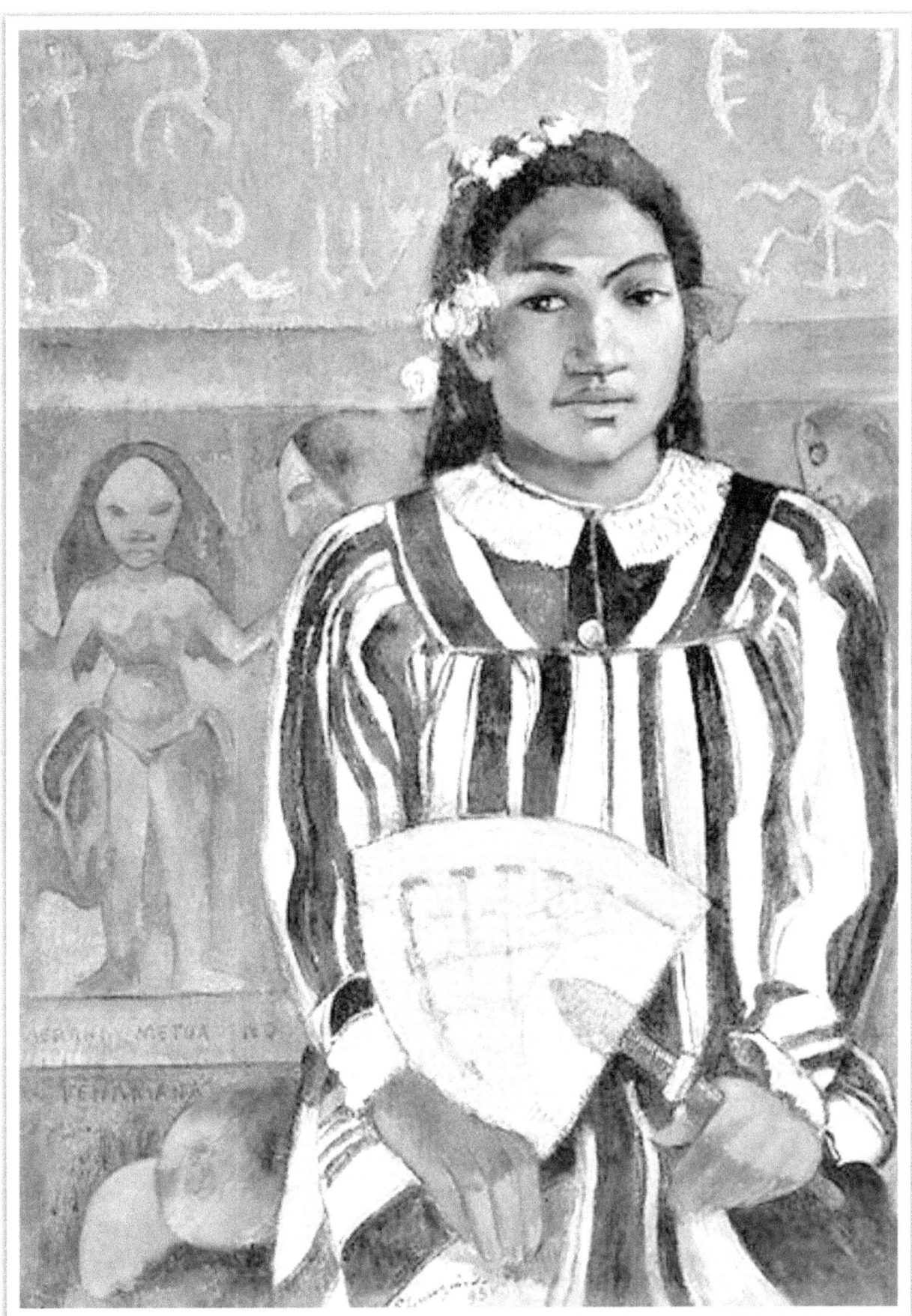

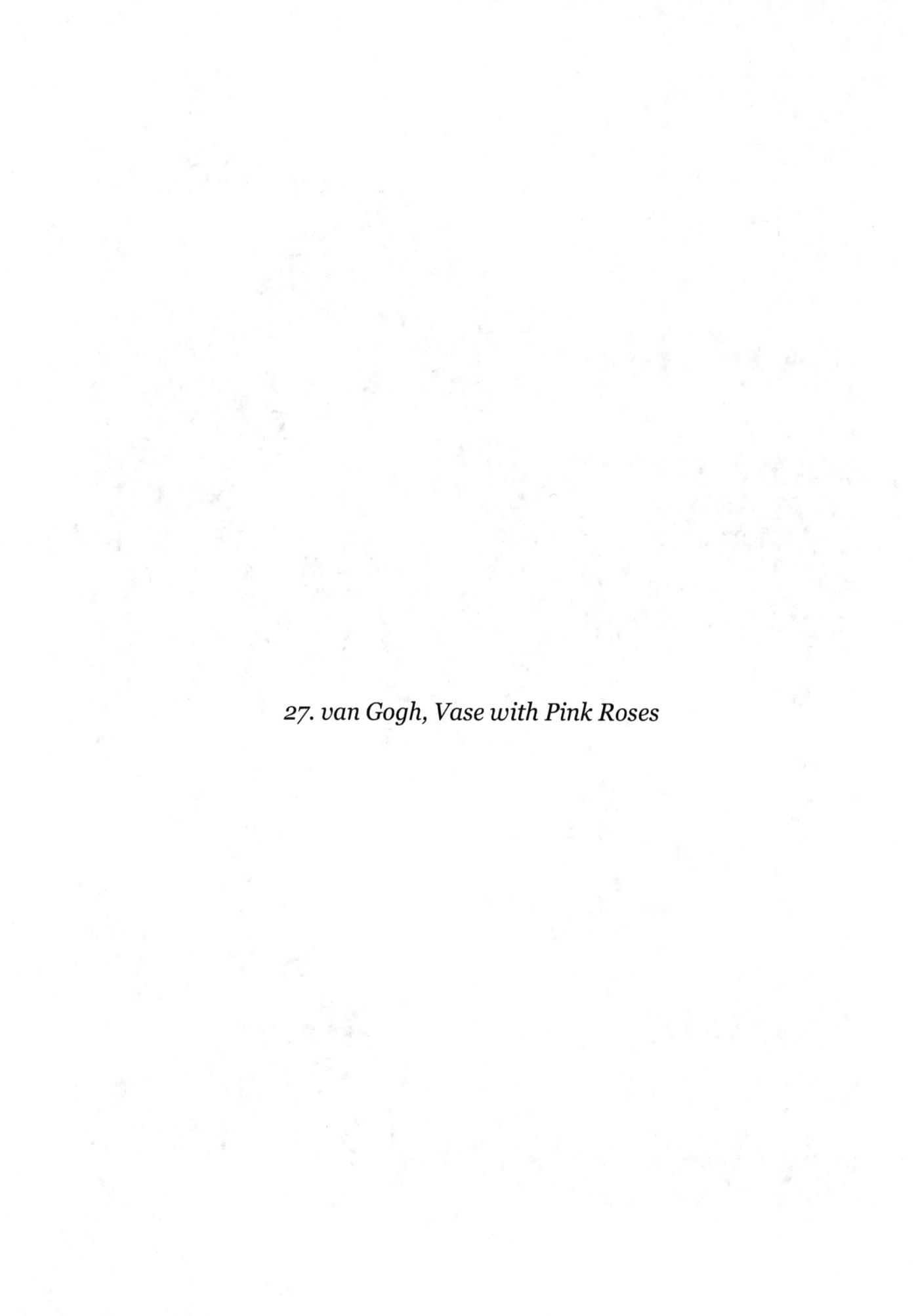

27. van Gogh, Vase with Pink Roses

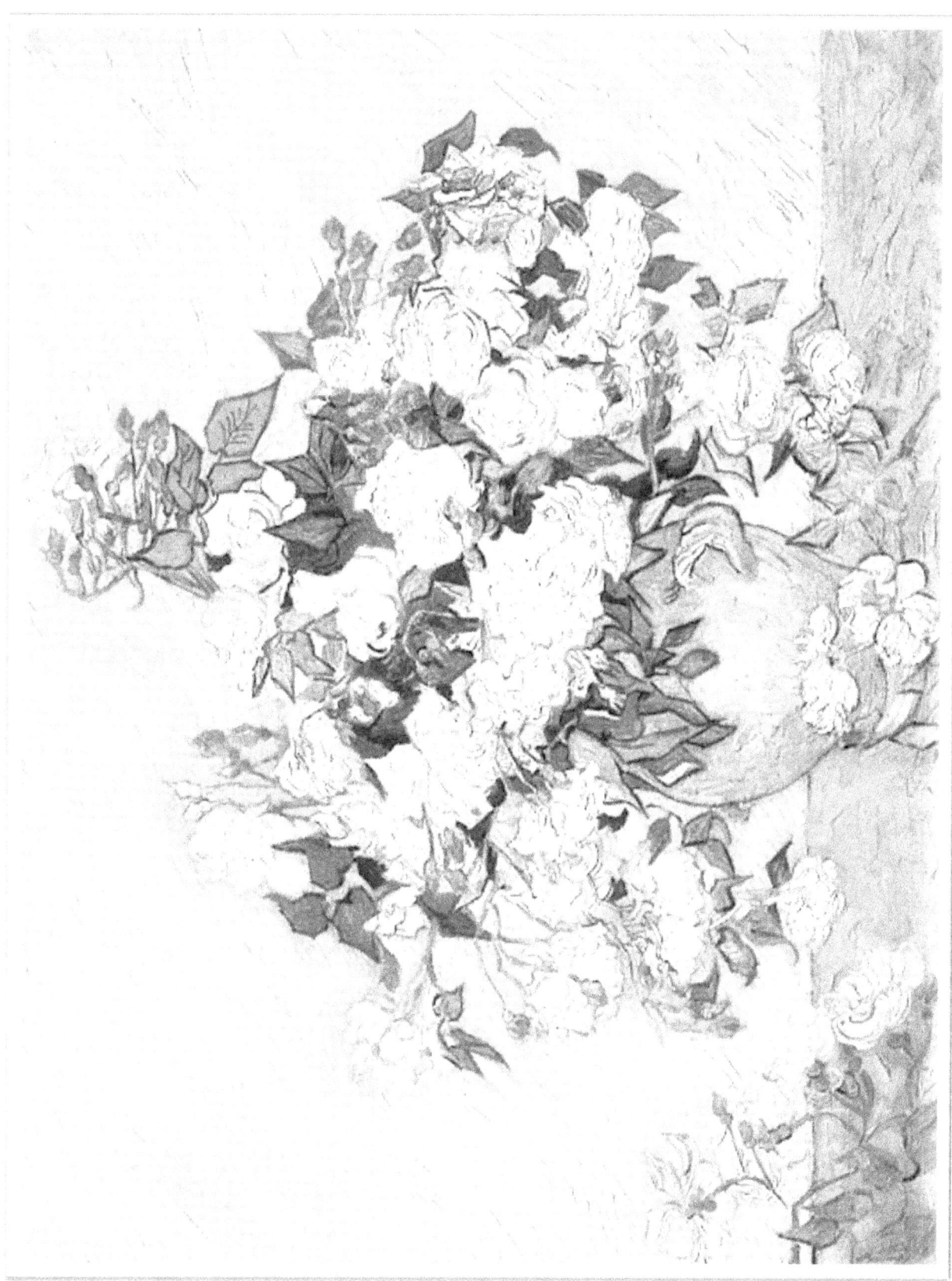

28. Lautrec, The Clowness at the Moulin Rouge

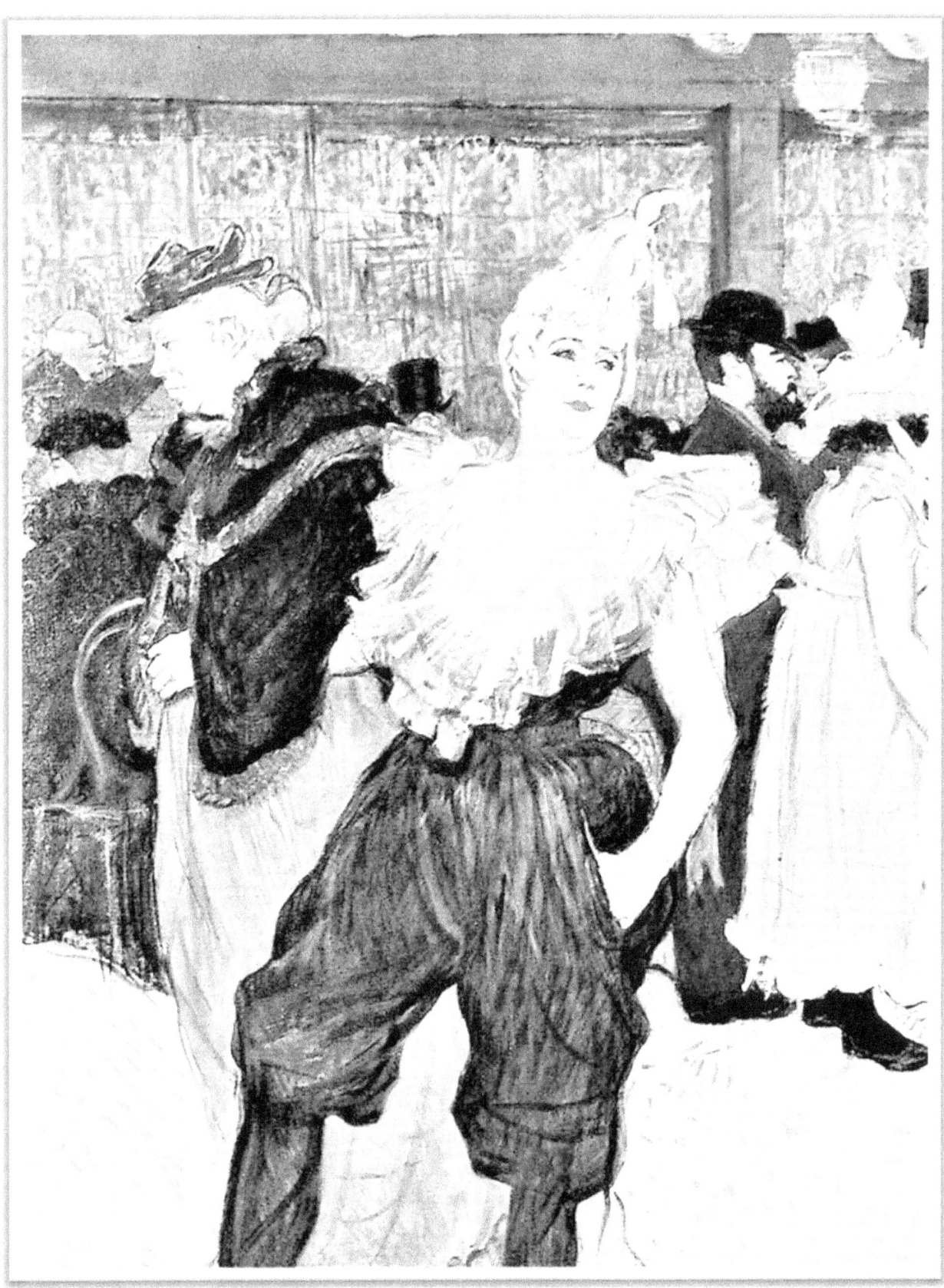

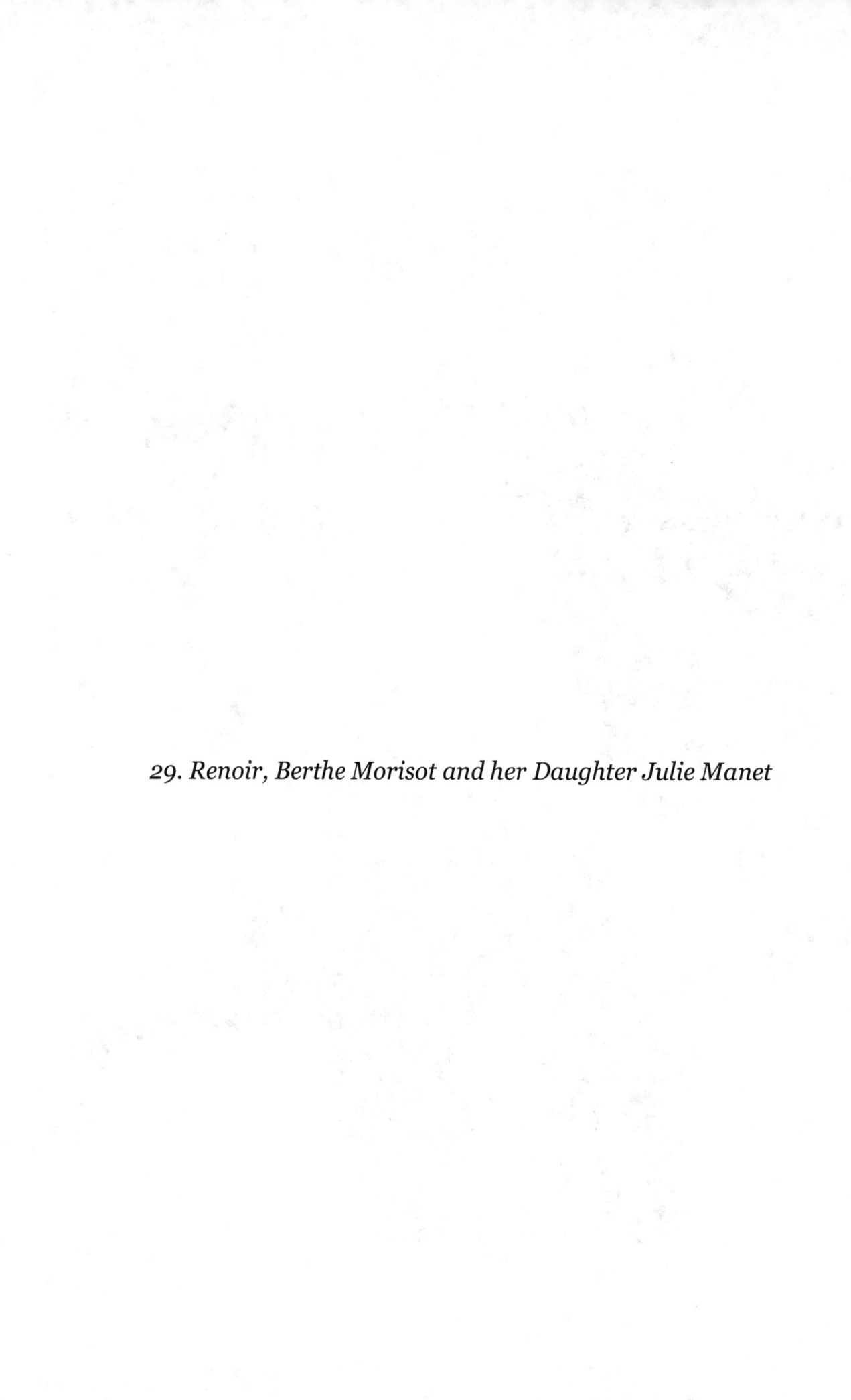

29. *Renoir, Berthe Morisot and her Daughter Julie Manet*

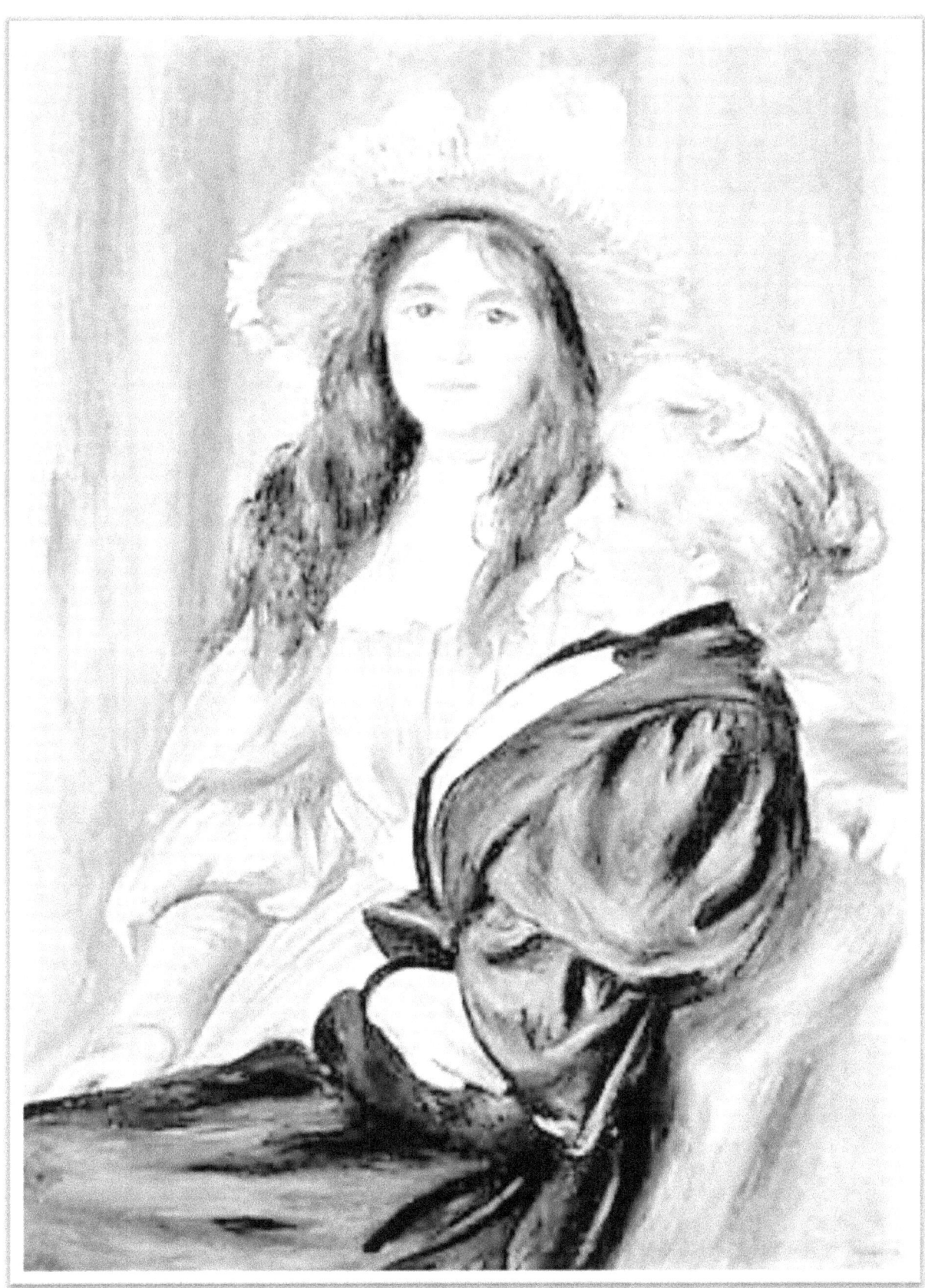

30. Lautrec, The Sofa

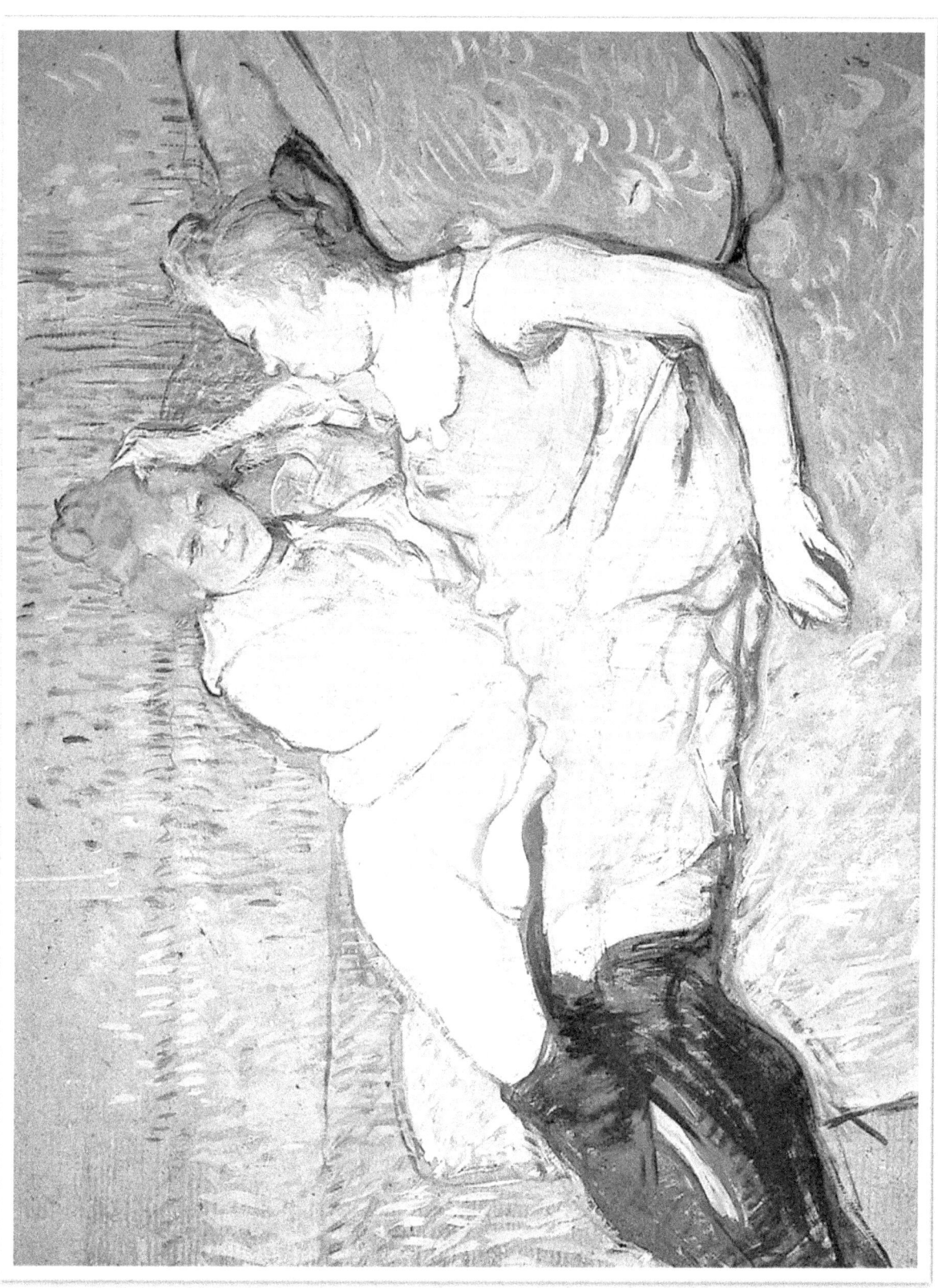

31. Degas, After the Bath, Woman Drying Herself

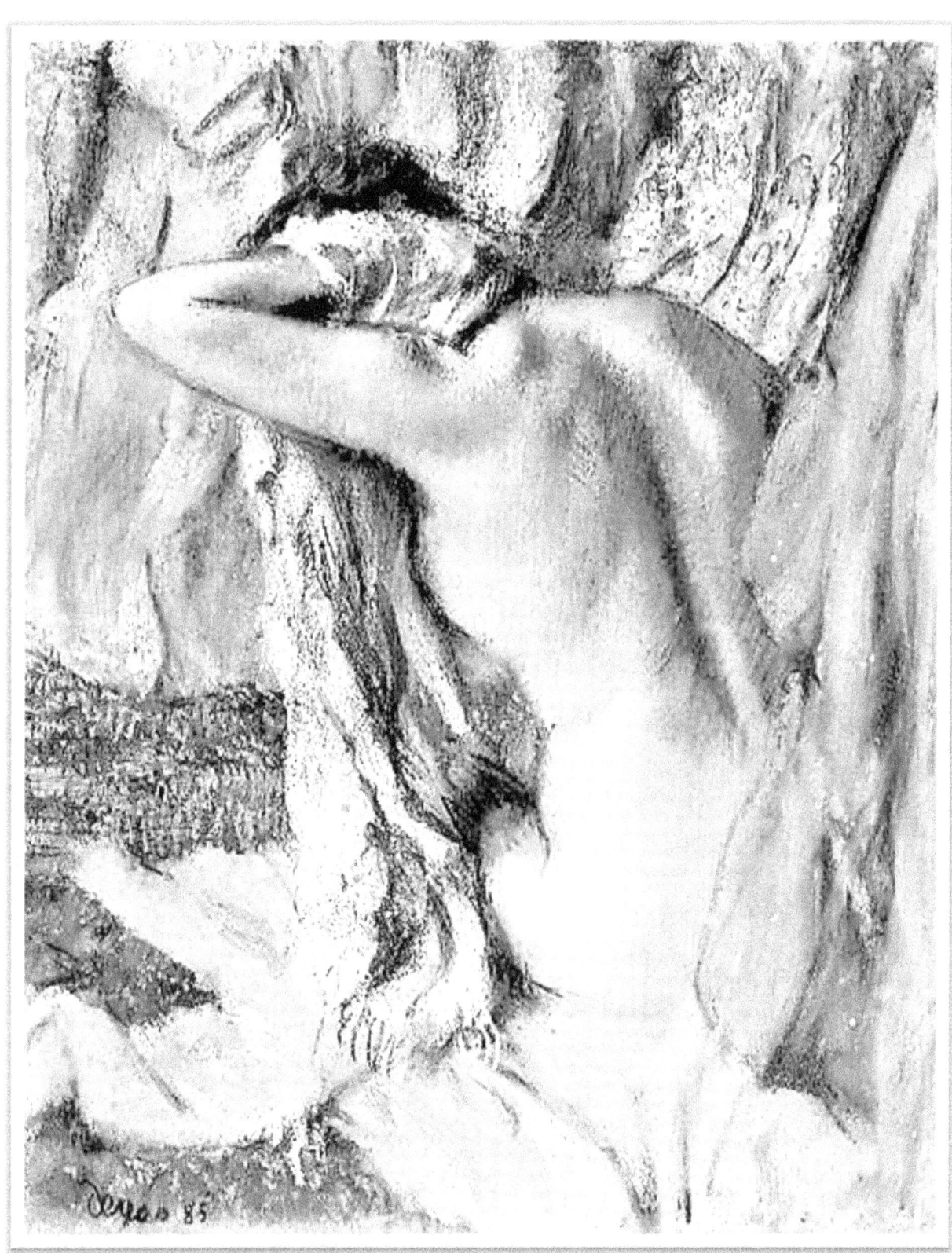

32. Berthe Morisot (1841-1895), The Pink Dress

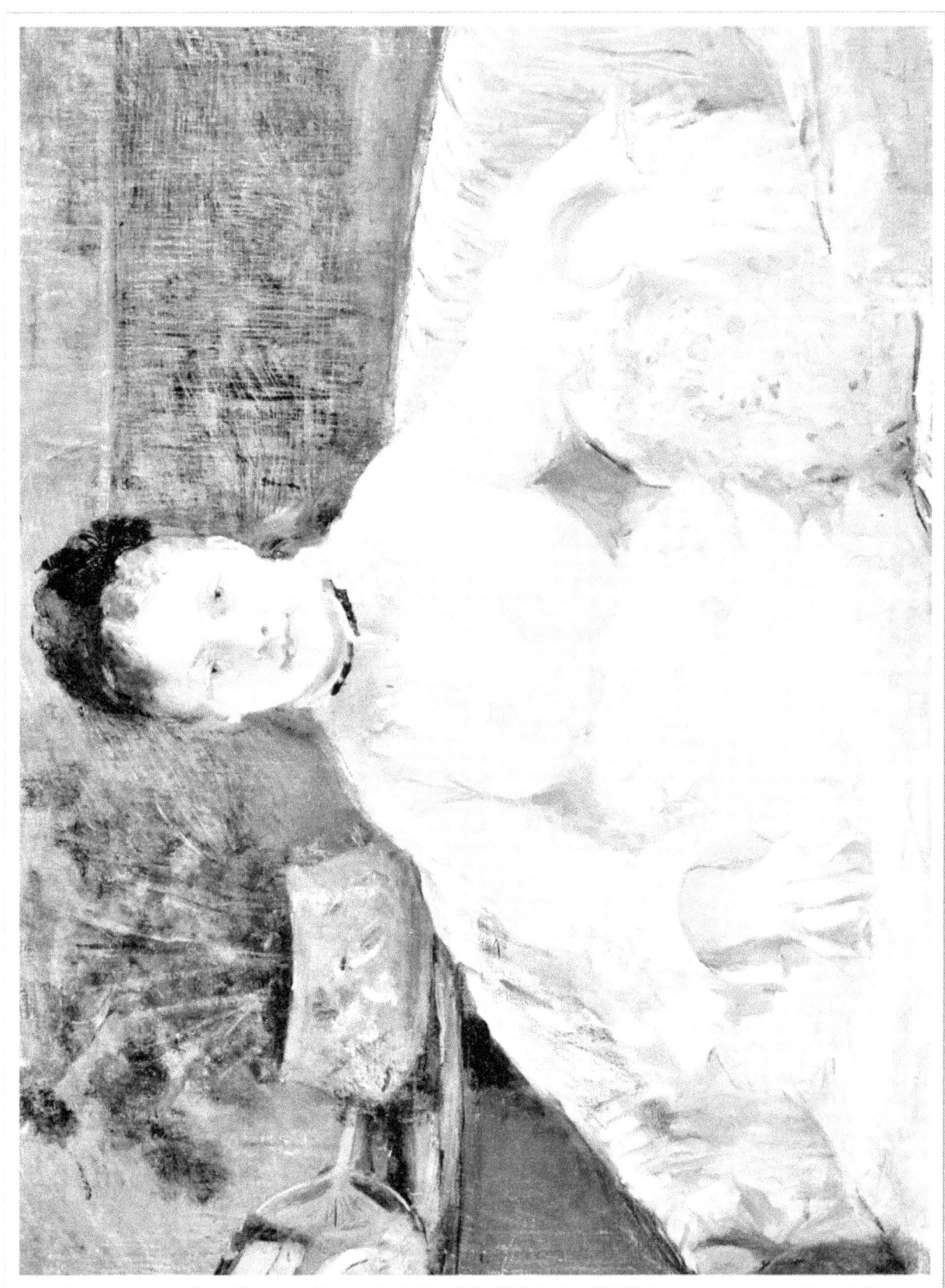

33. Cassatt, Lady at the Tea Table

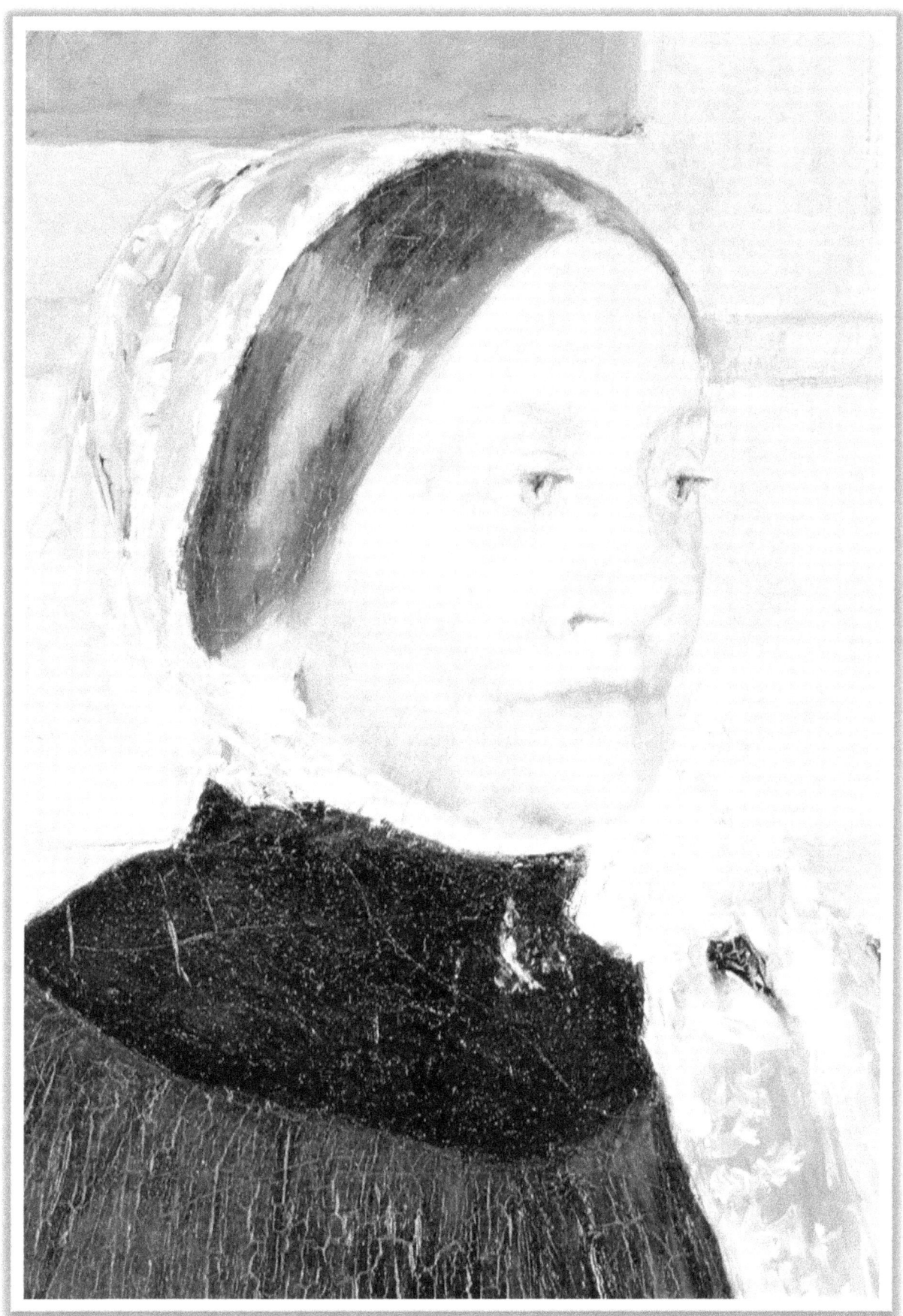

34. van Gogh, Small Pear Tree in Blossom

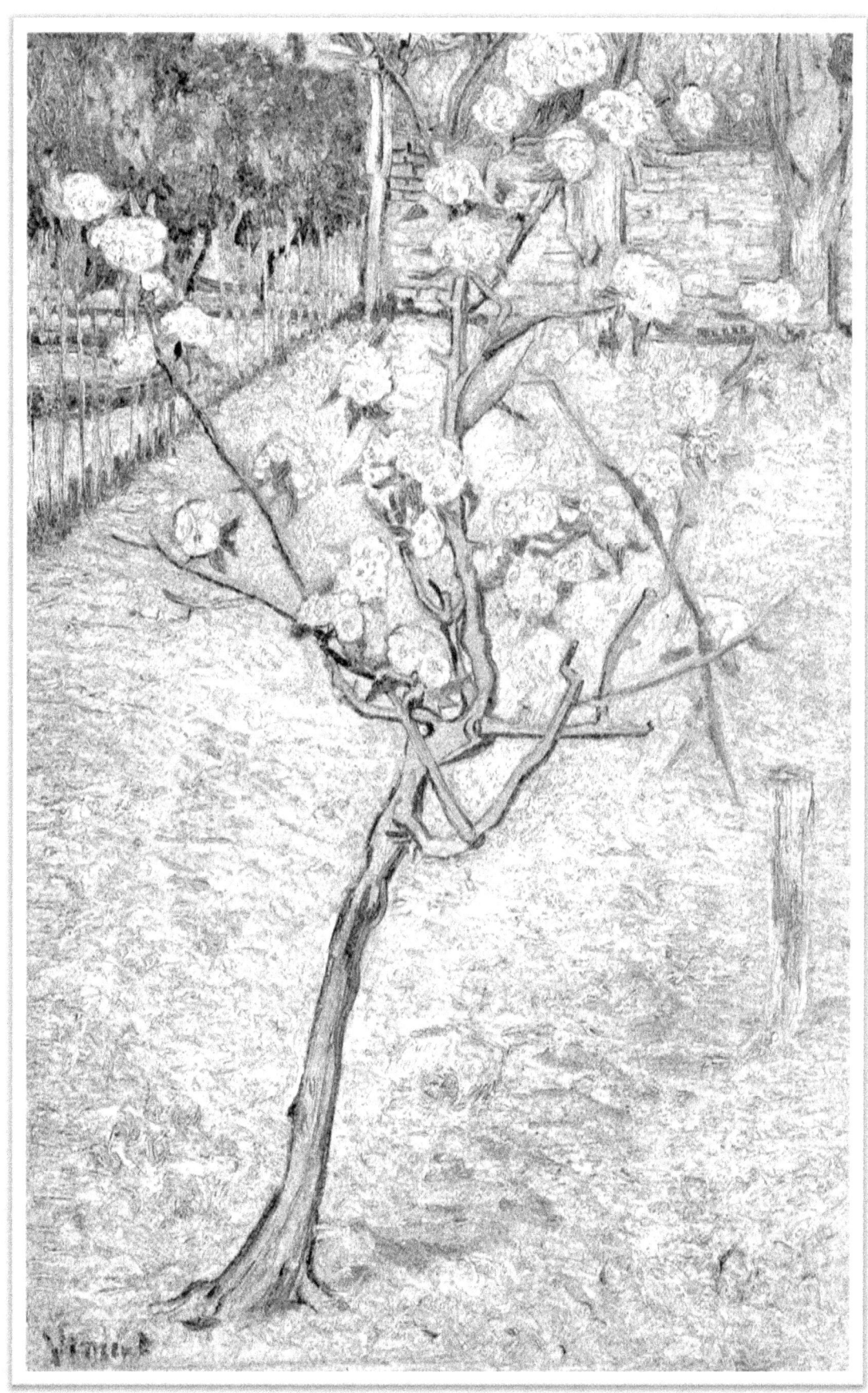

35. van Gogh, Flower Fields in Holland, Bulb Fields

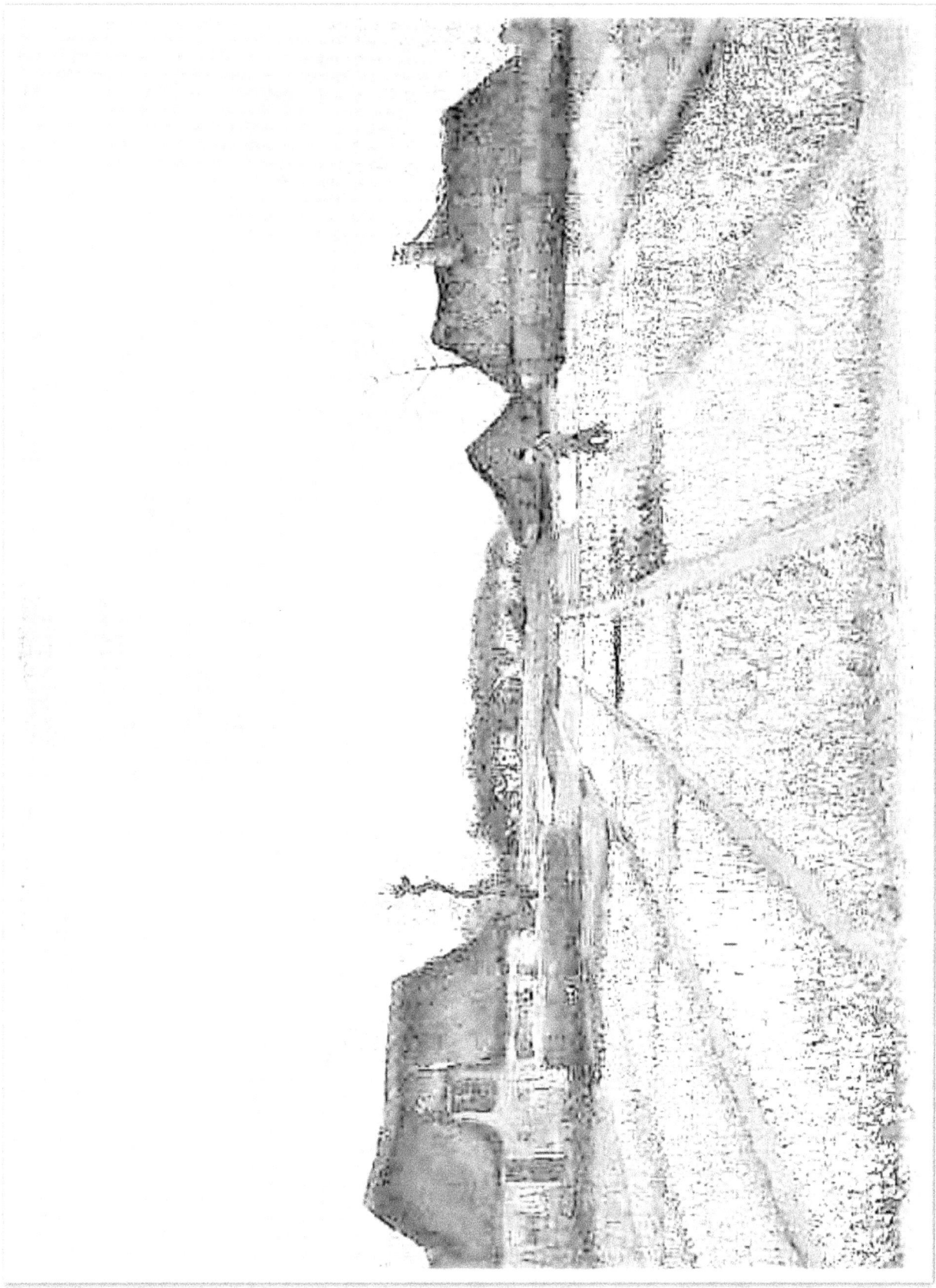

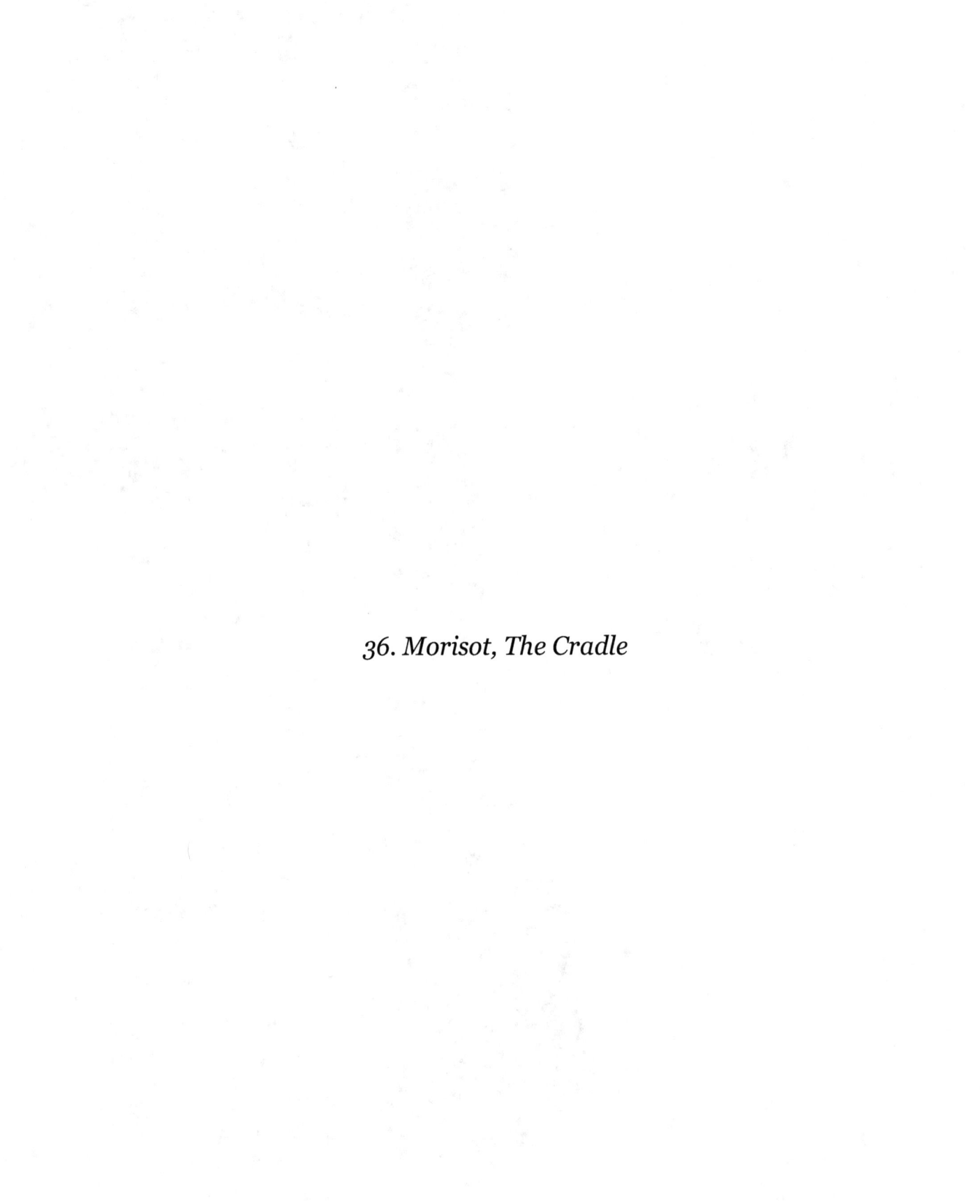

36. Morisot, The Cradle

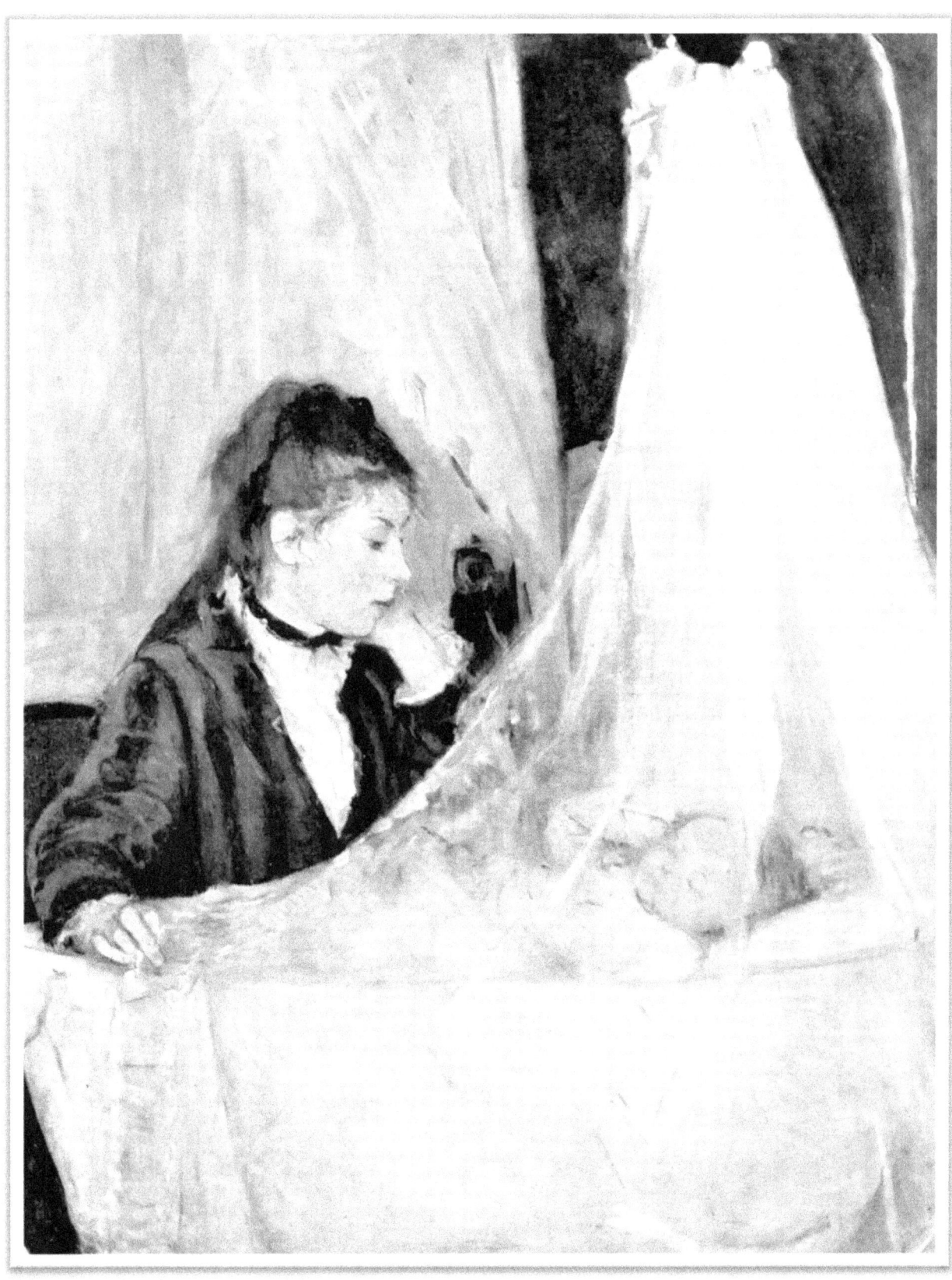

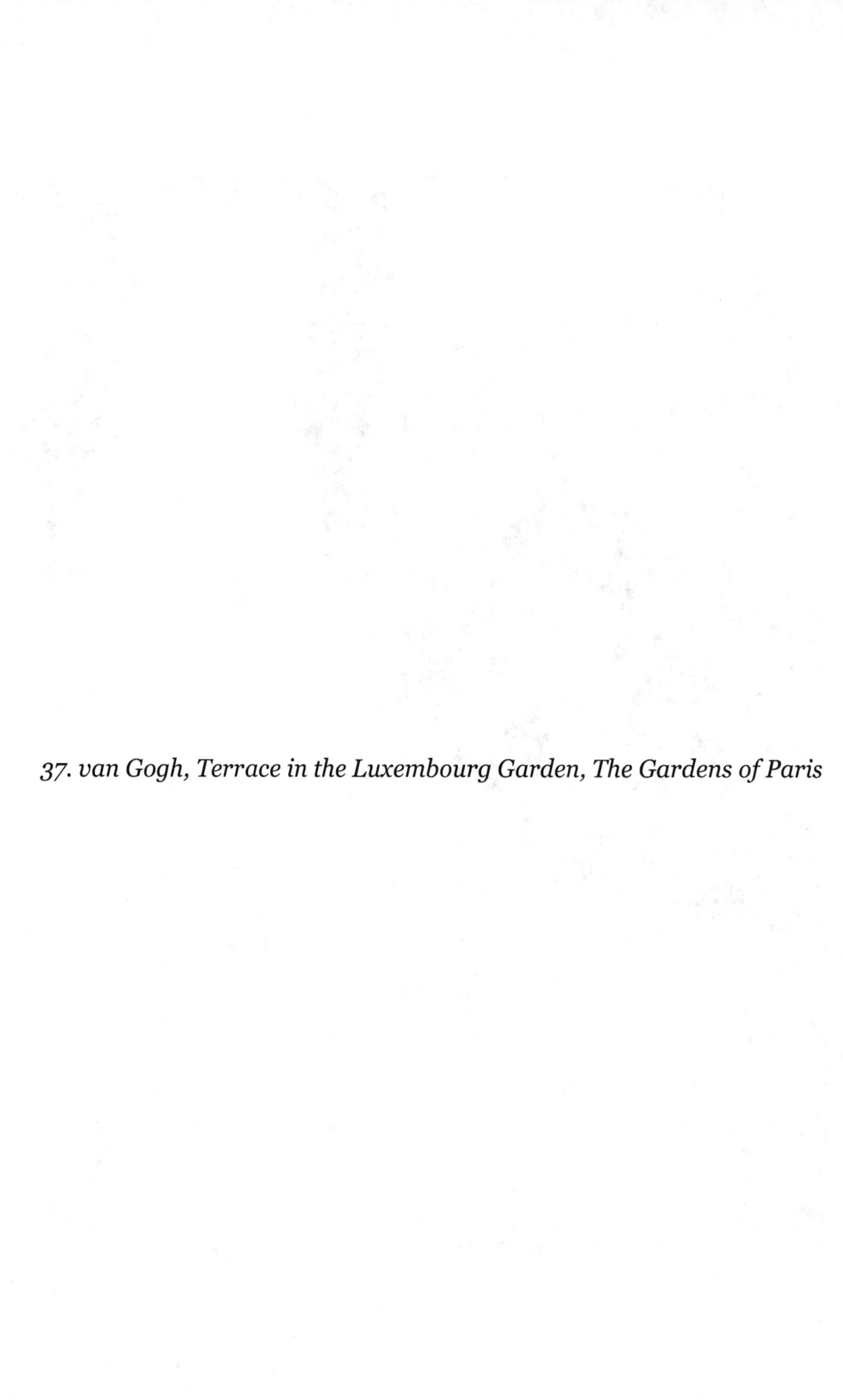

37. van Gogh, *Terrace in the Luxembourg Garden, The Gardens of Paris*

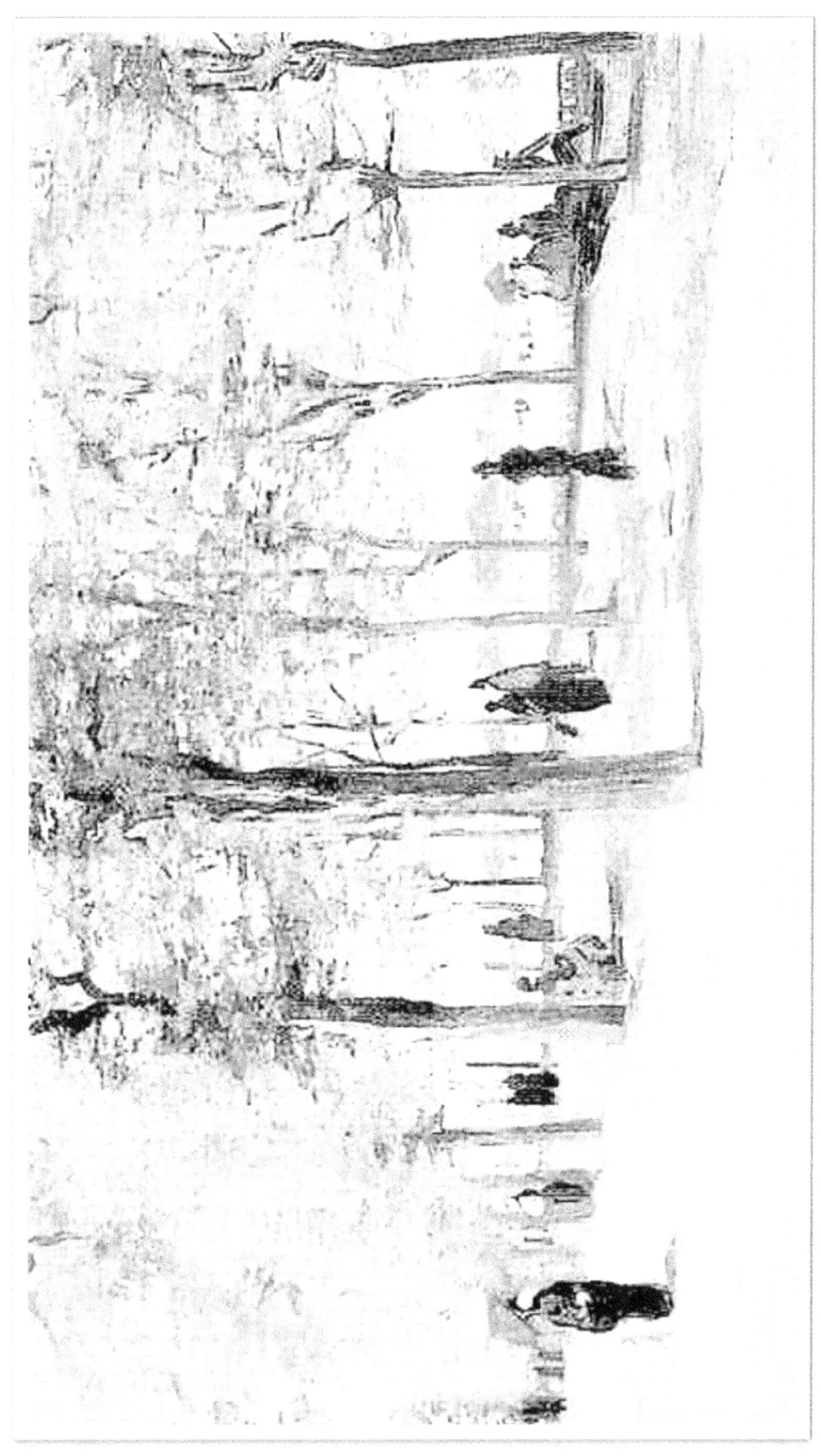

38. van Gogh, Lane in Voyer d'Argenson Park Asnières

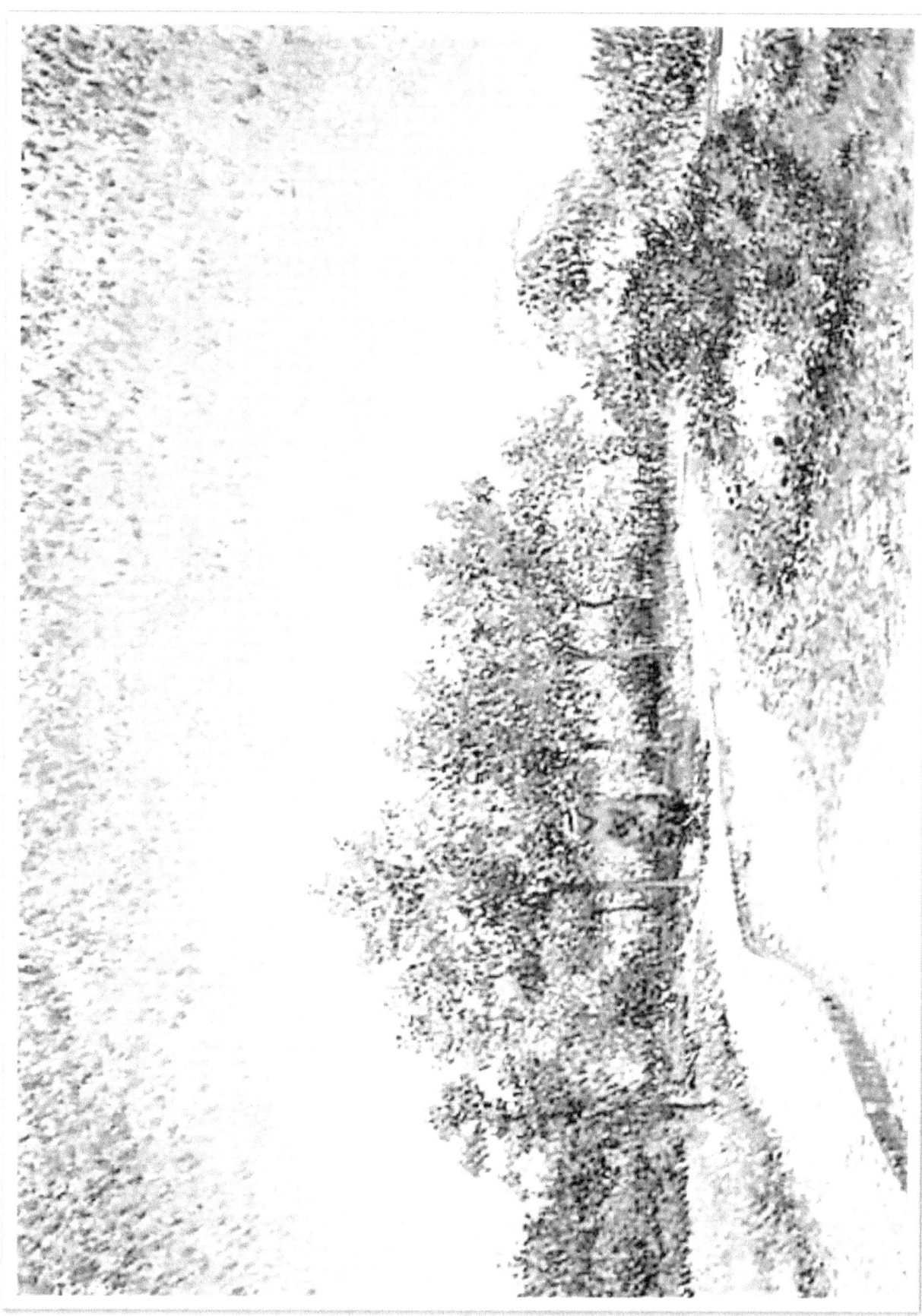

39. Degas, Before the Curtain Call

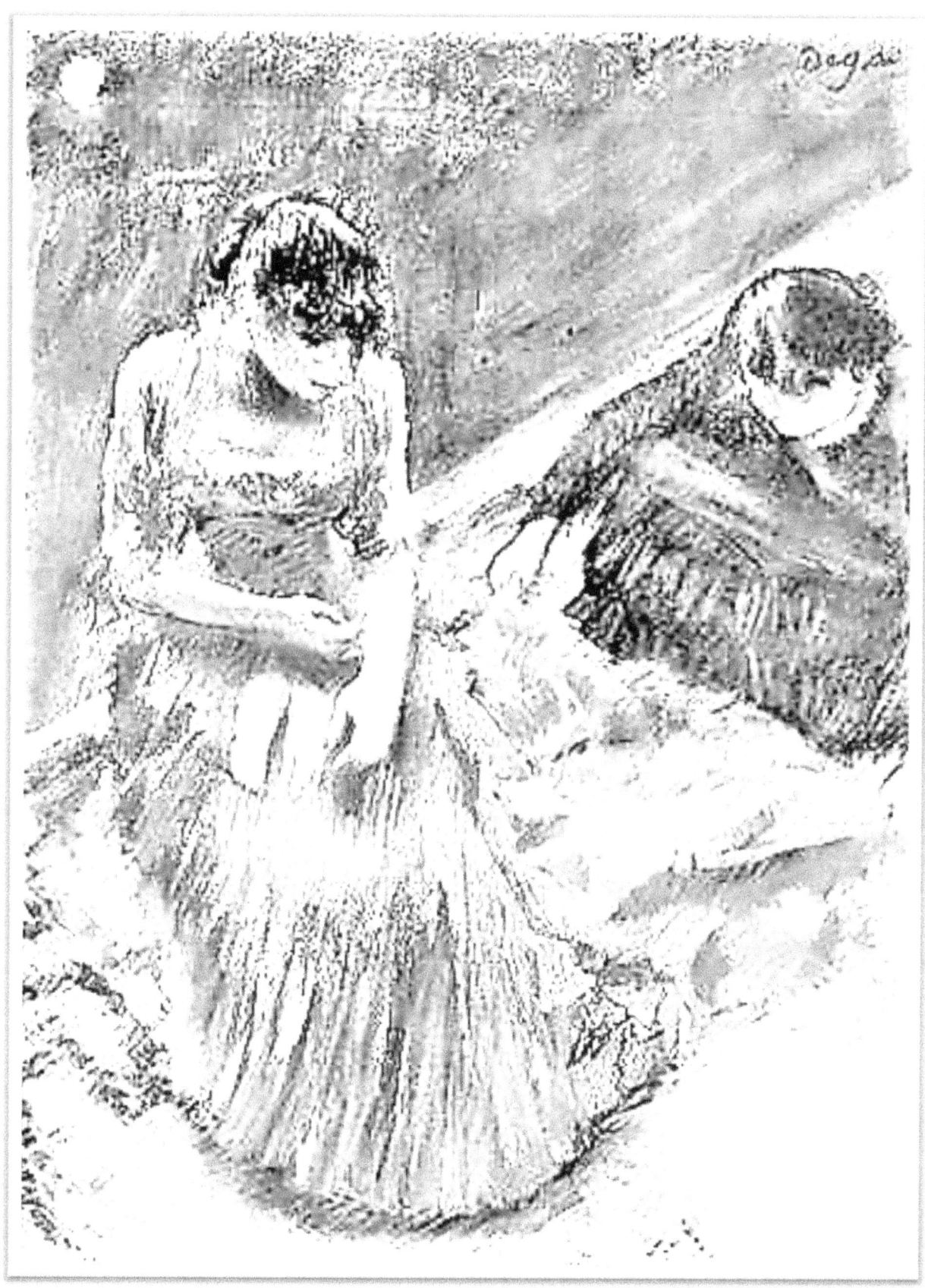

40. van Gogh, Factories at Asnières

41. Cassatt, Young Mother Sewing

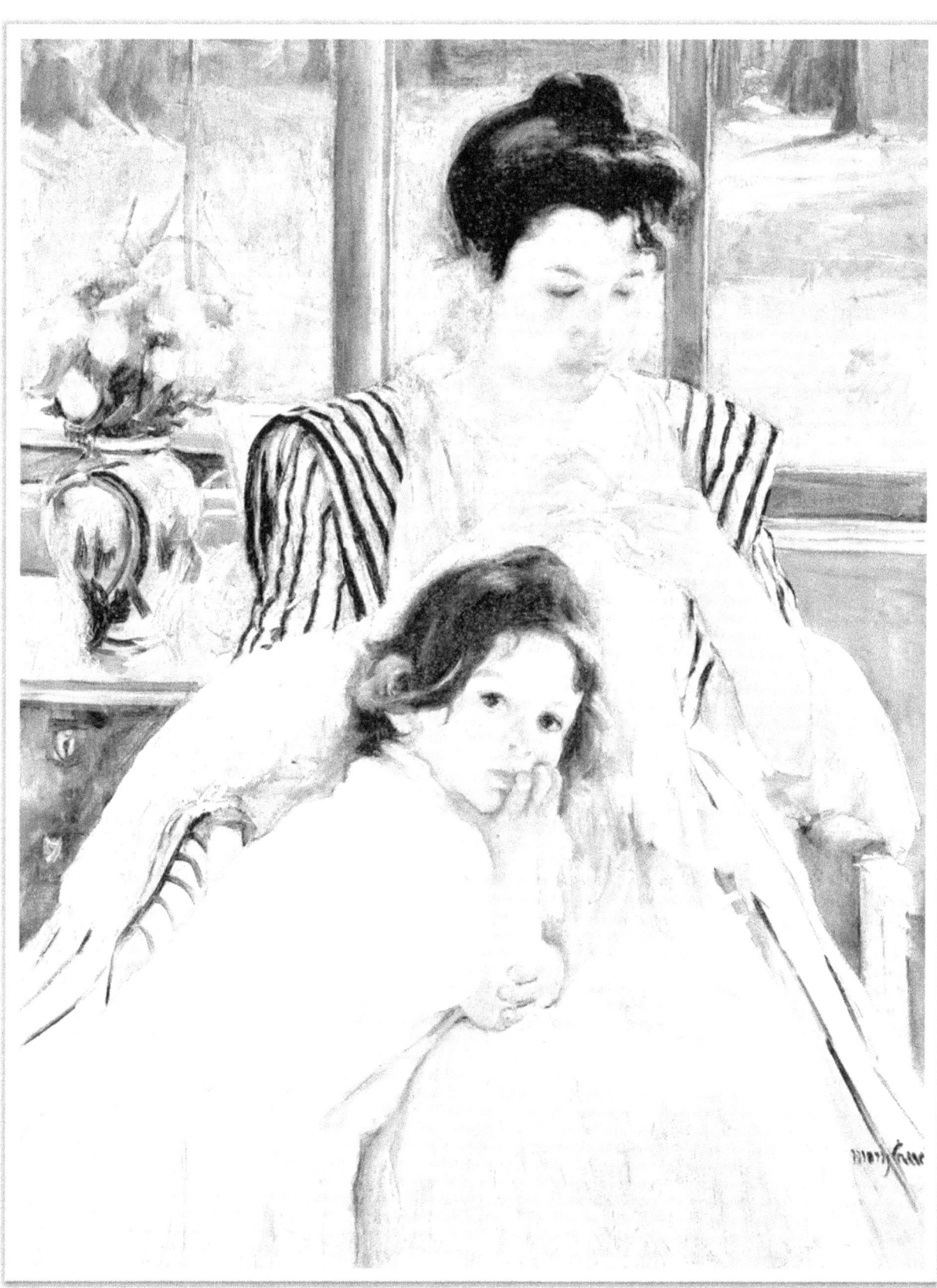

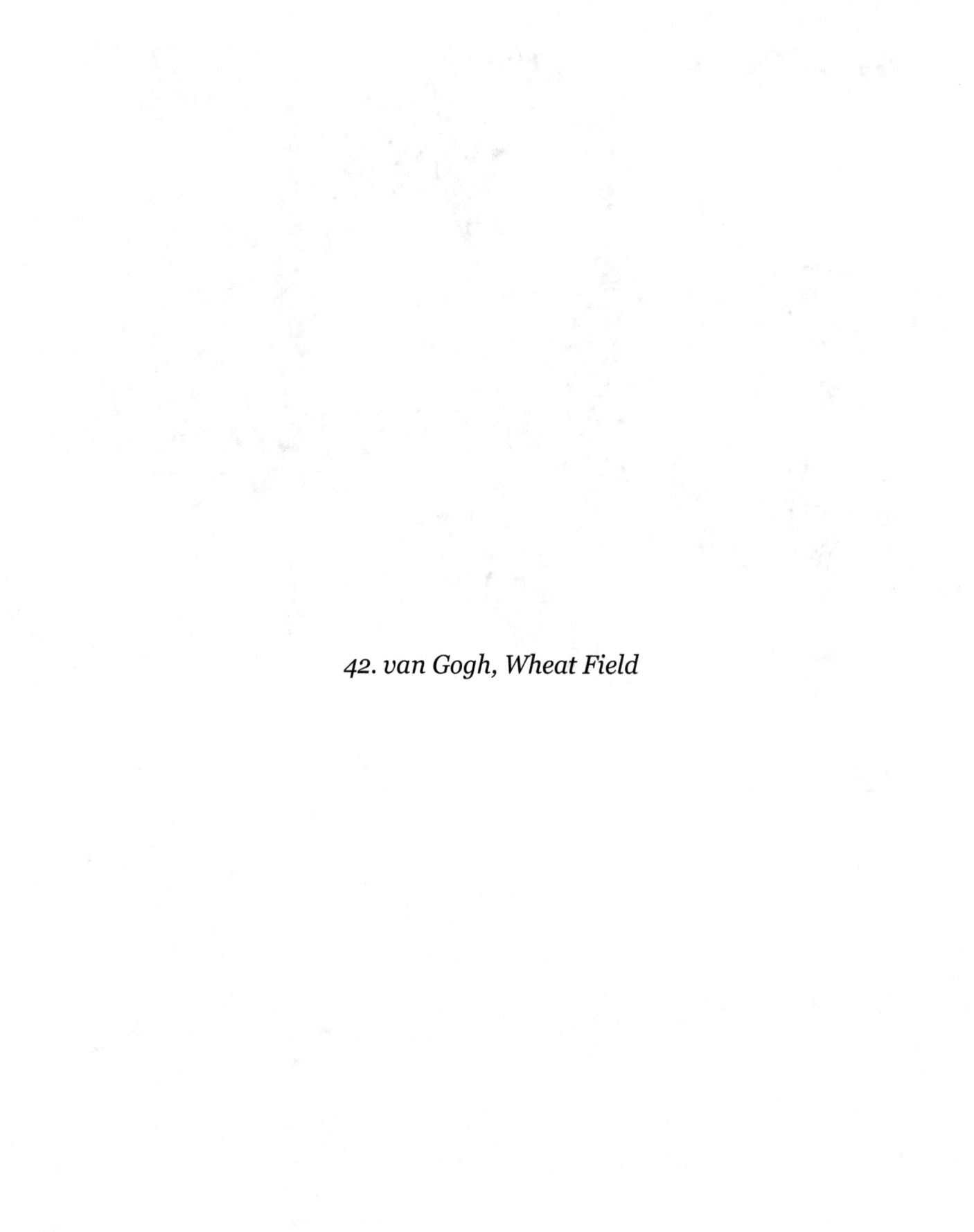

42. van Gogh, Wheat Field

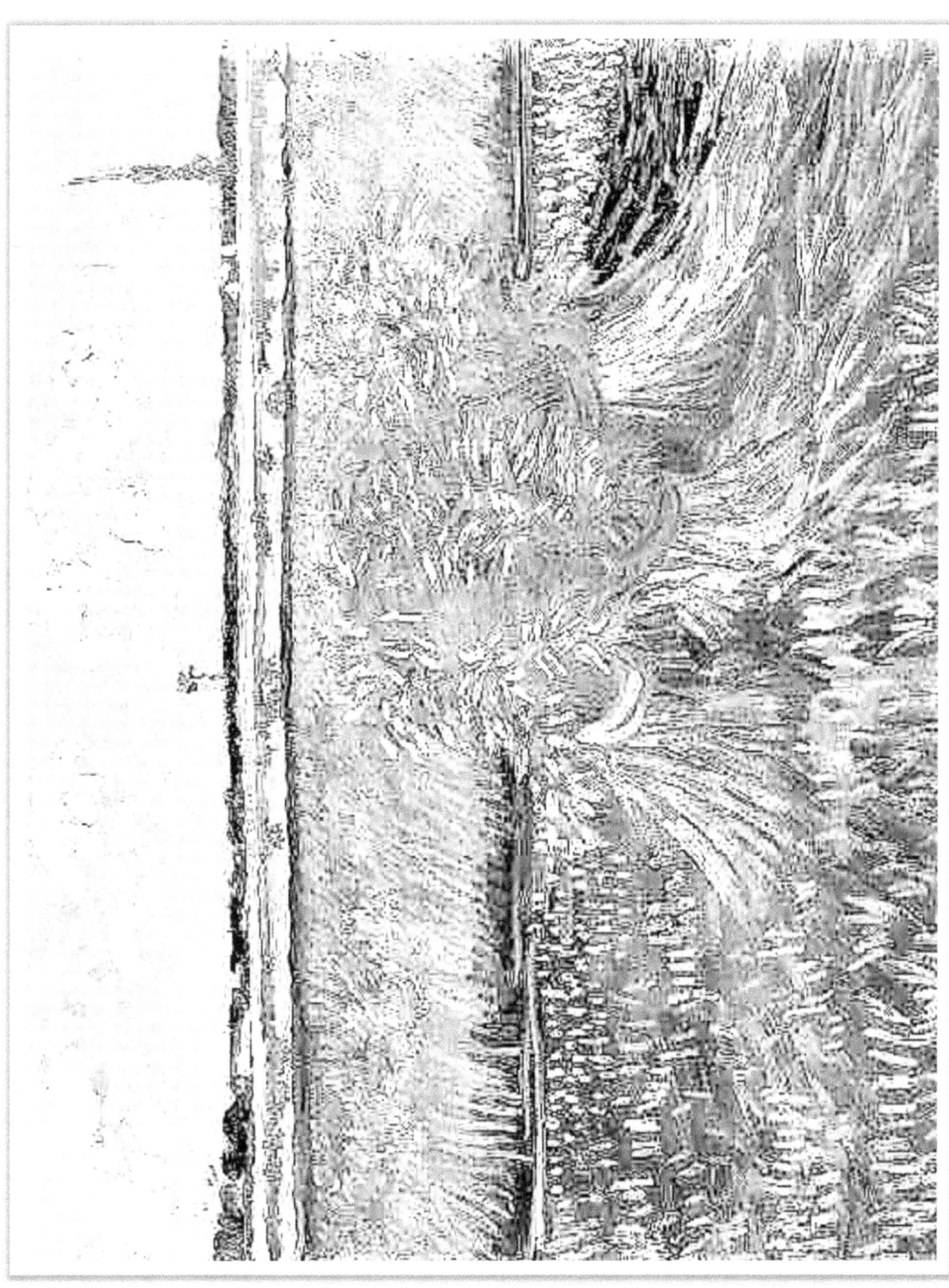

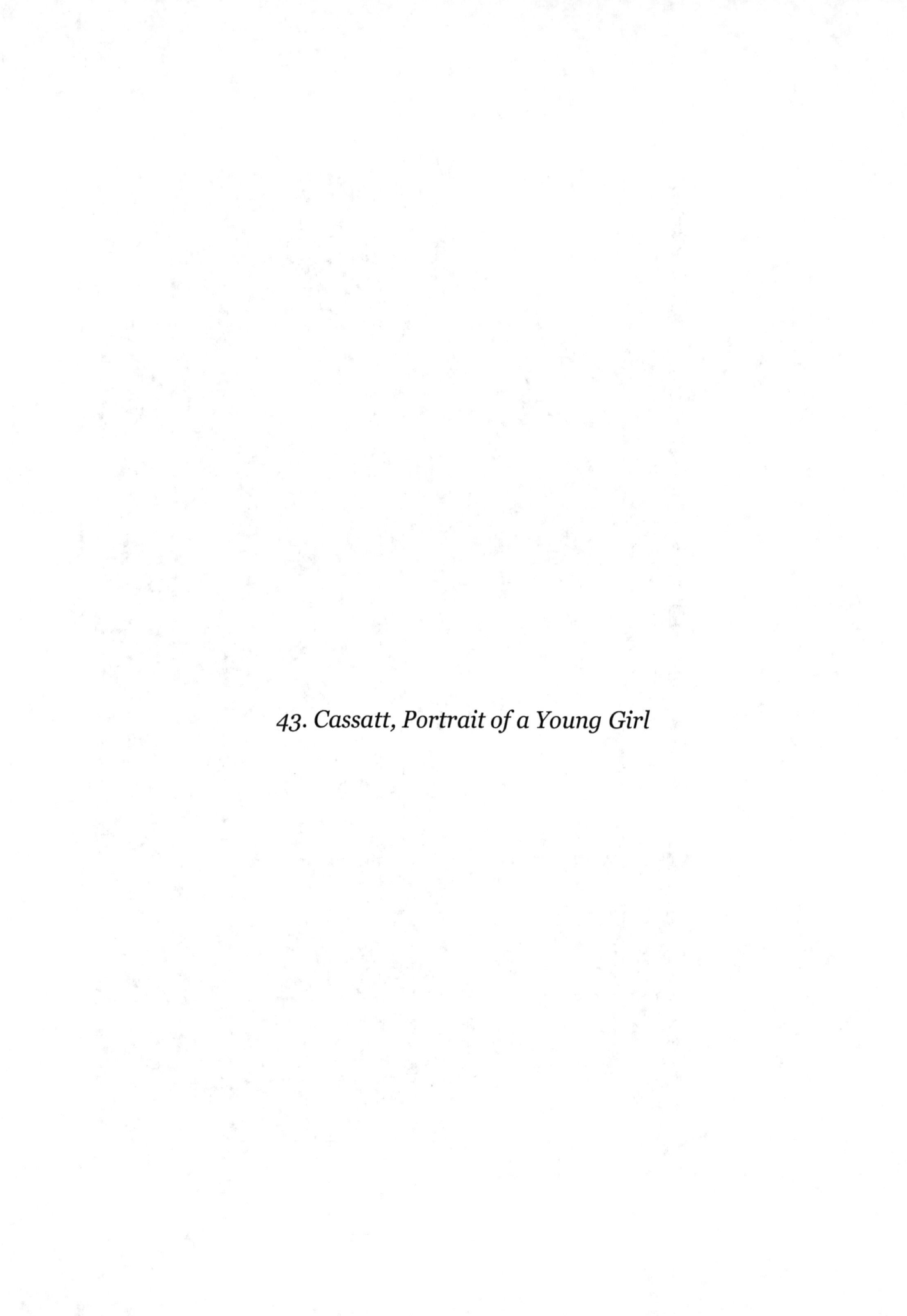

43. Cassatt, Portrait of a Young Girl

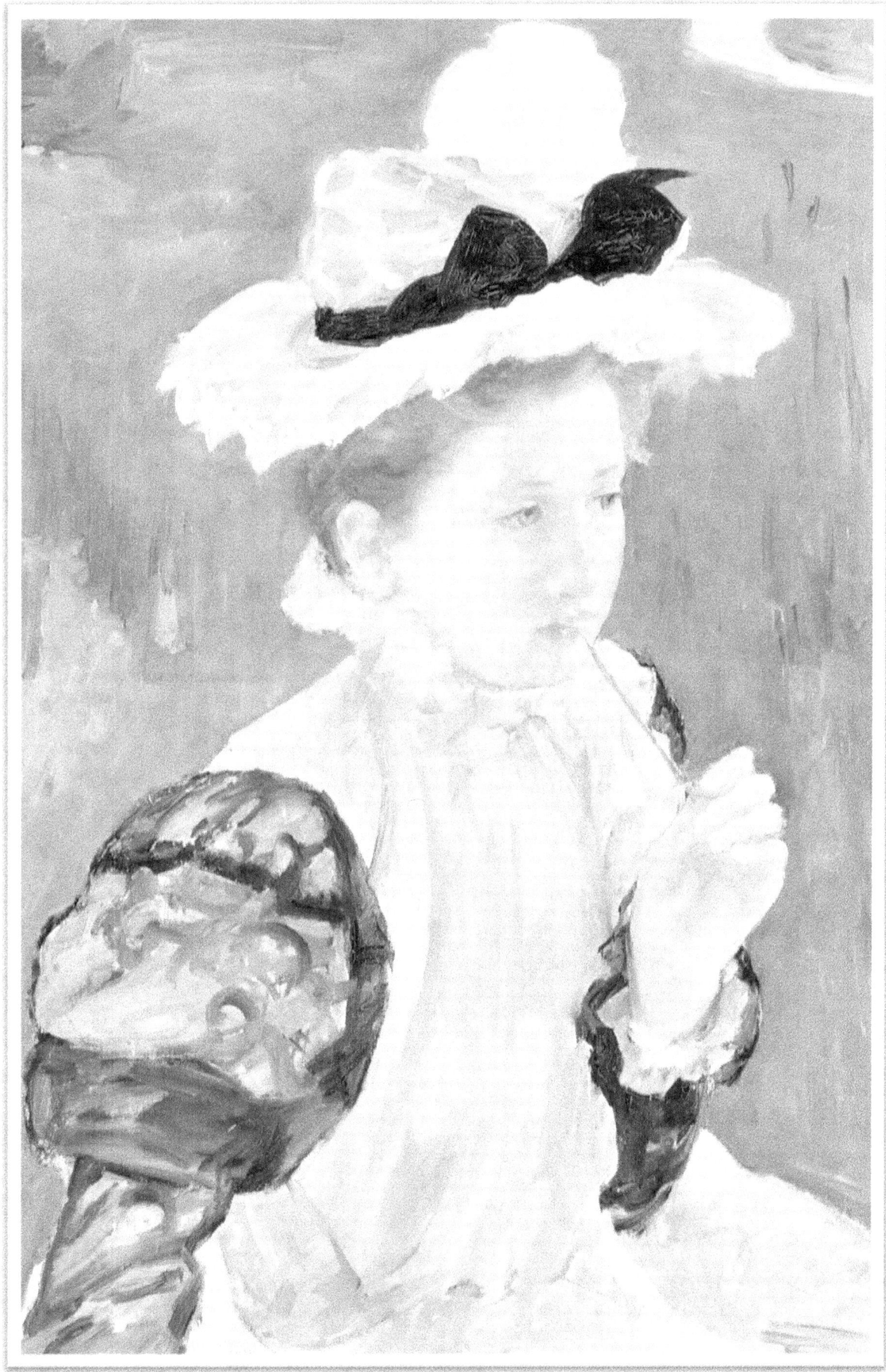

44. van Gogh, The Brothel

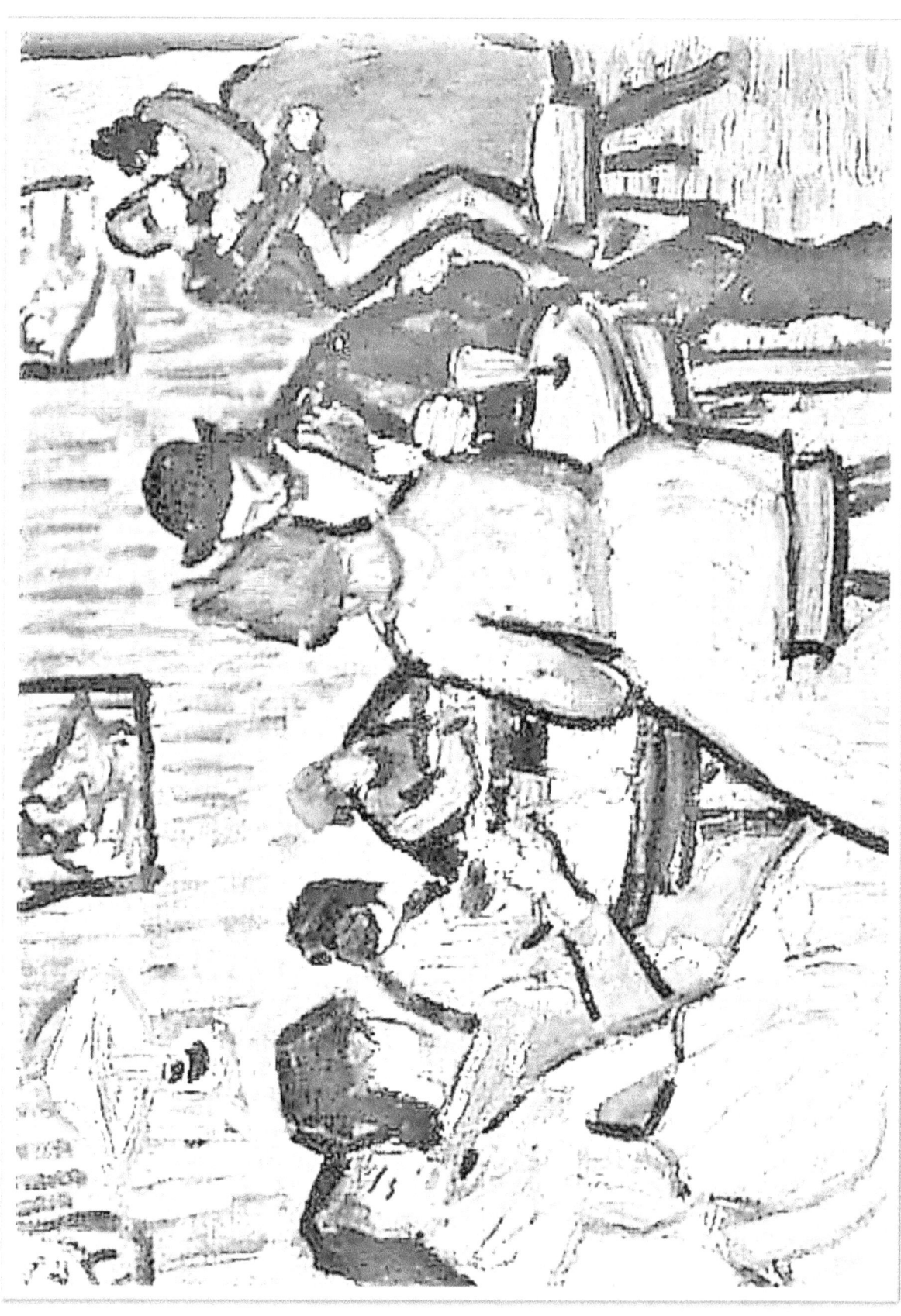

45. Manet, Mademoiselle Isabelle Lemonnier

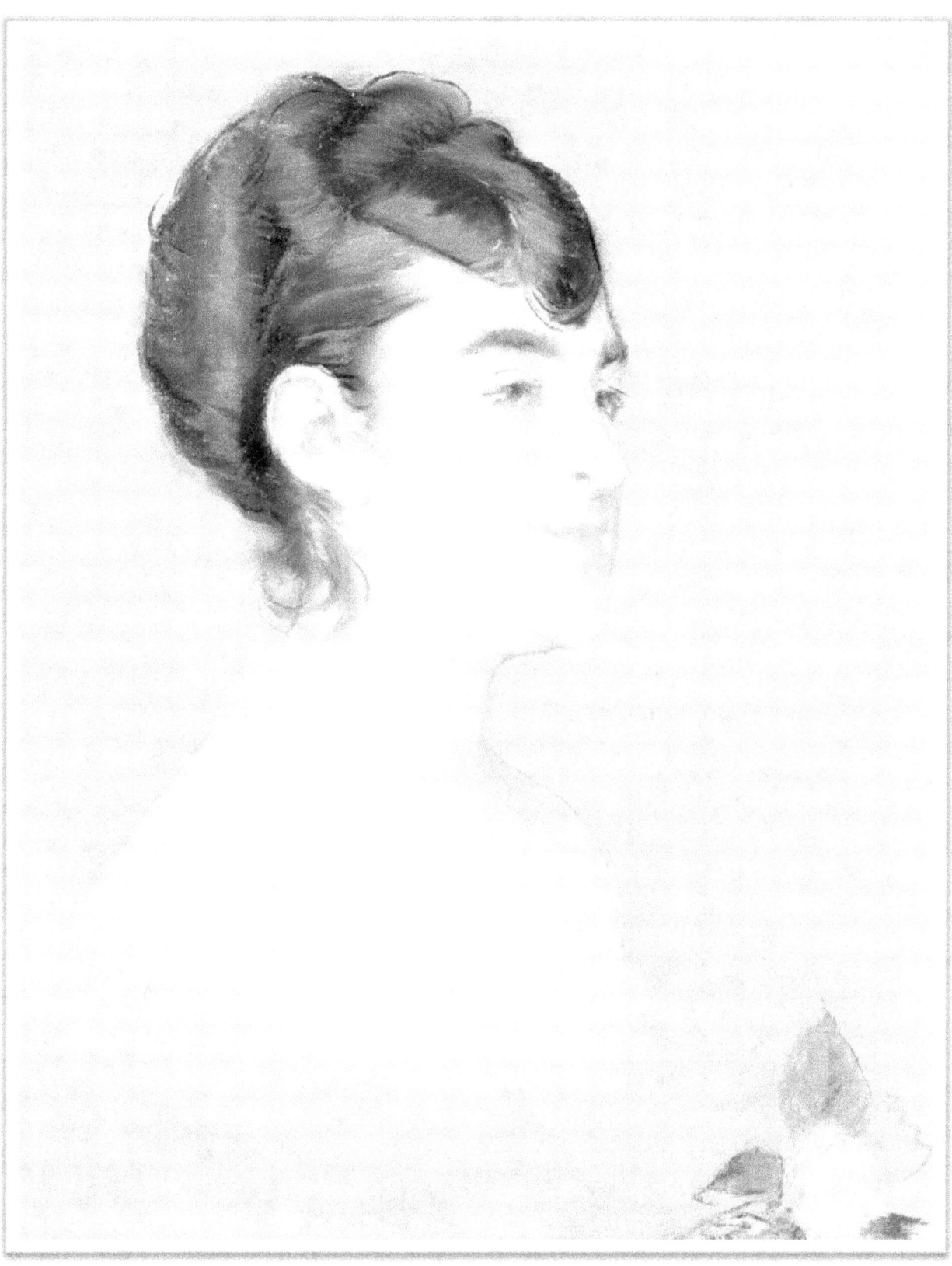

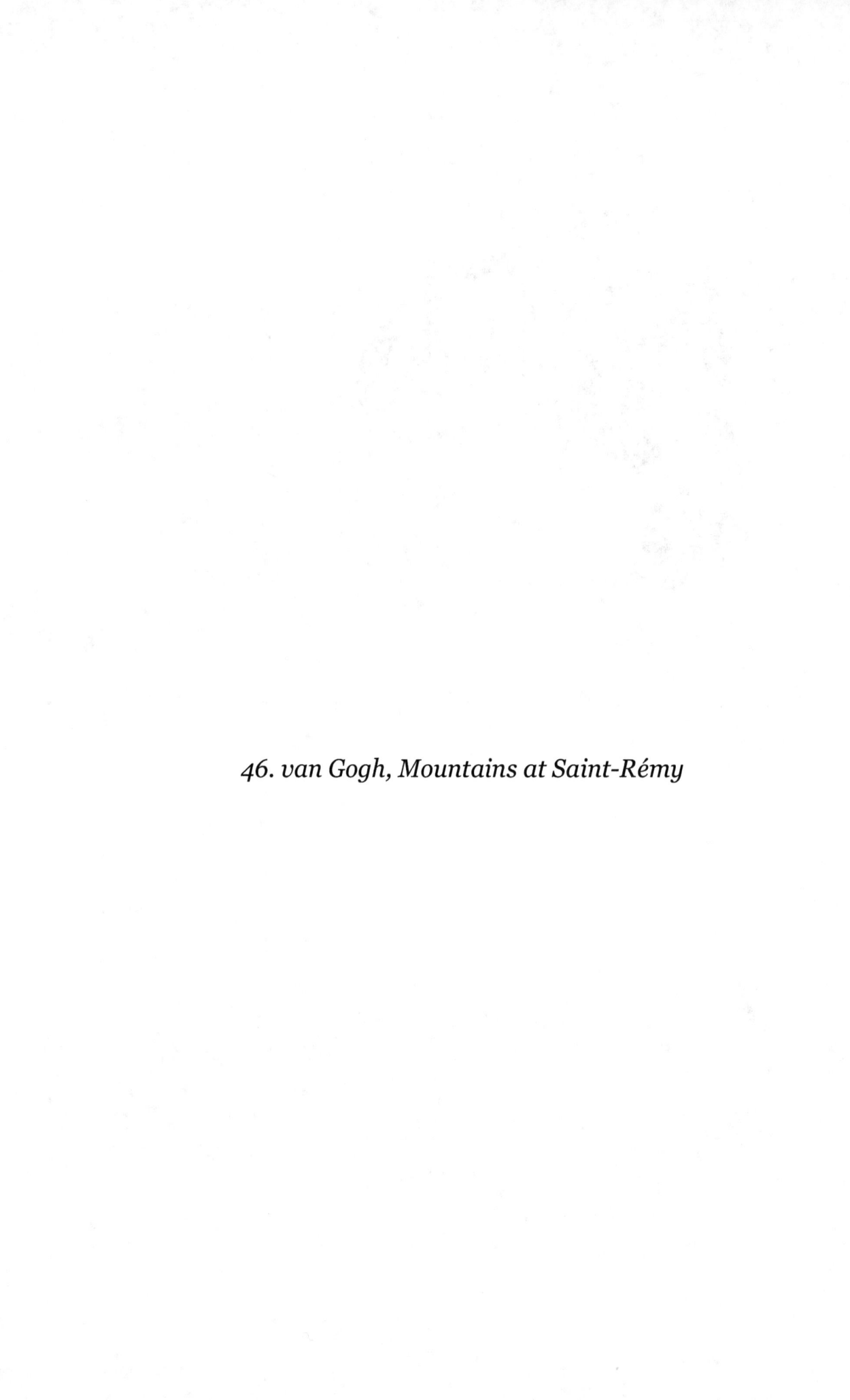

46. van Gogh, Mountains at Saint-Rémy

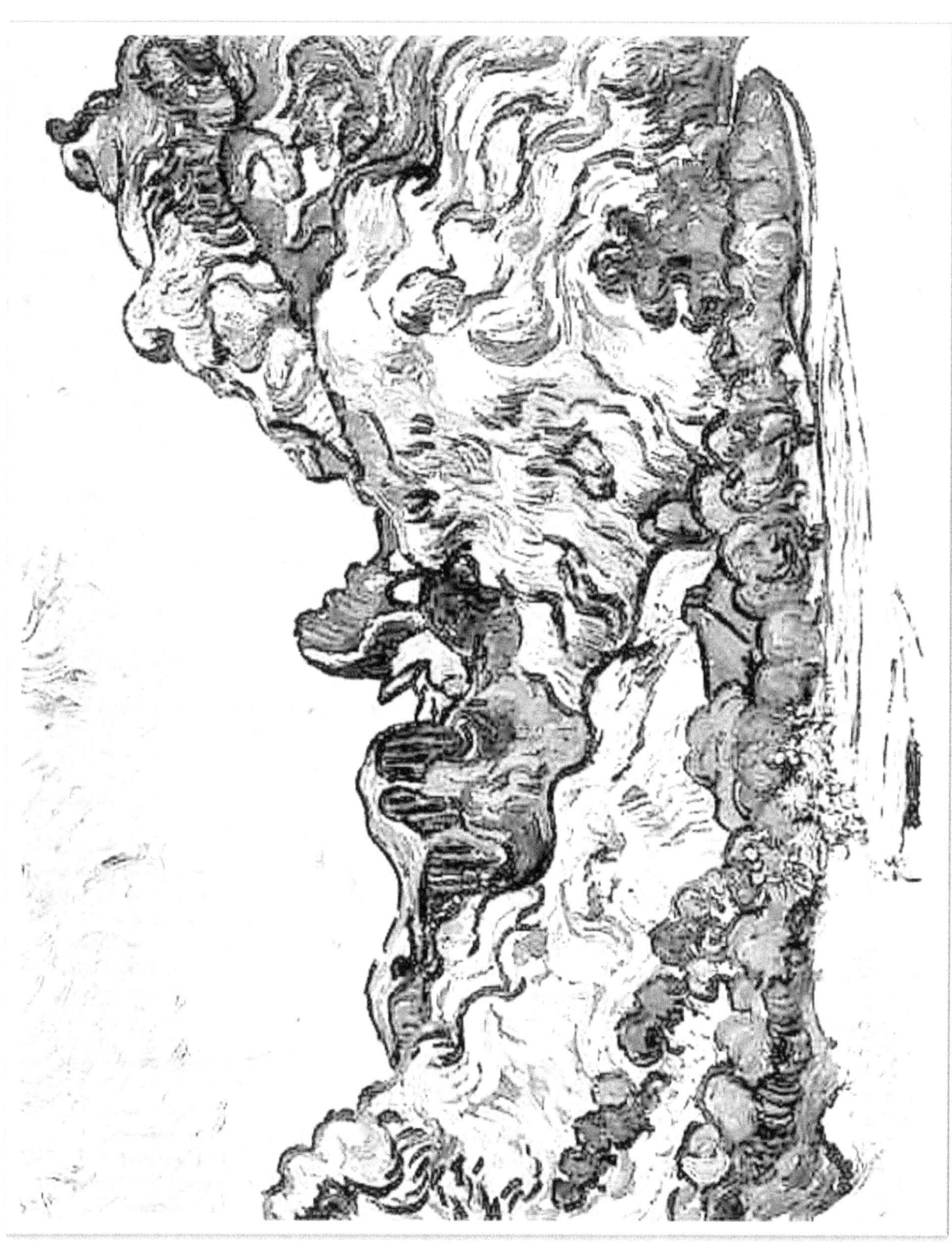

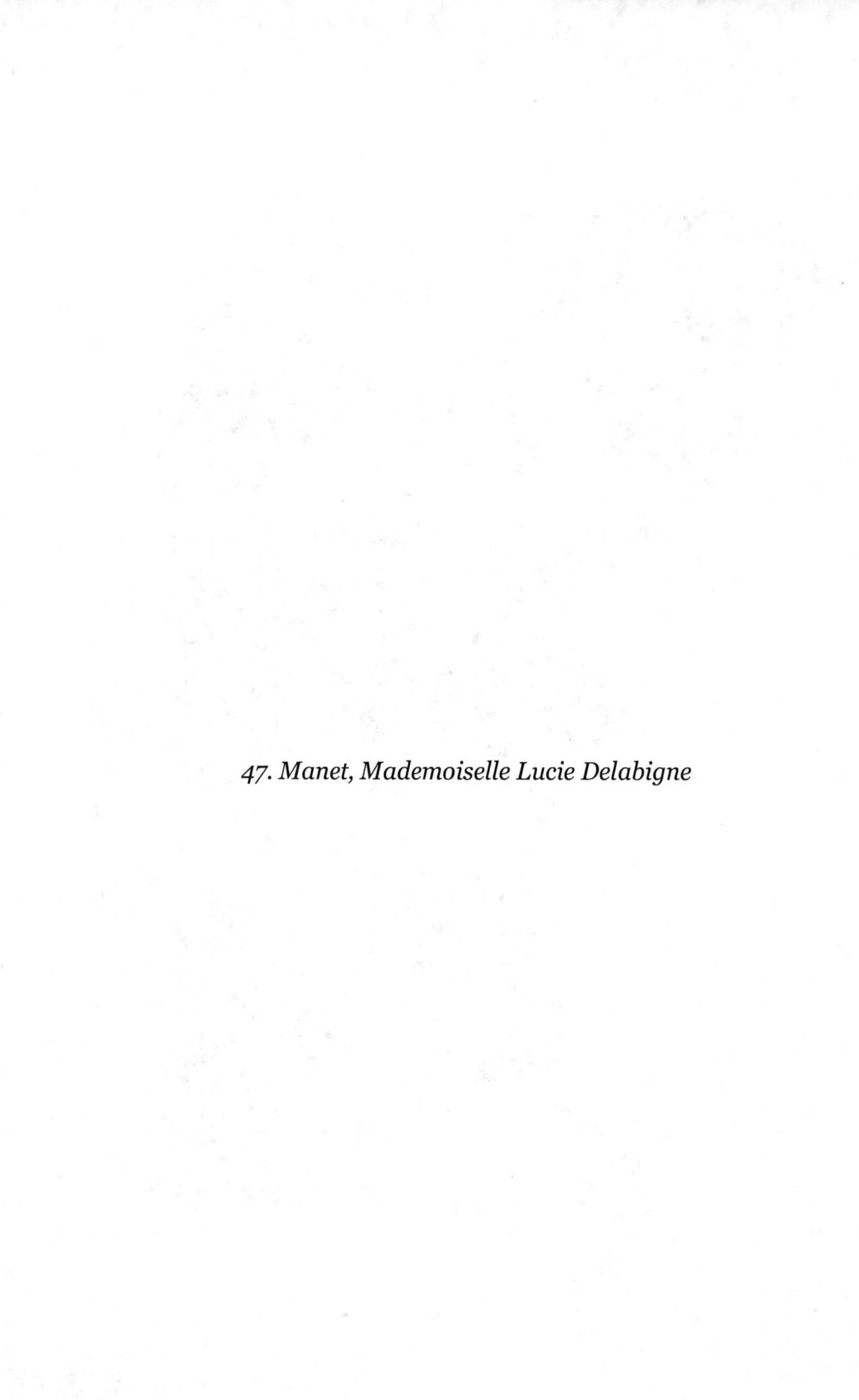

47. Manet, Mademoiselle Lucie Delabigne

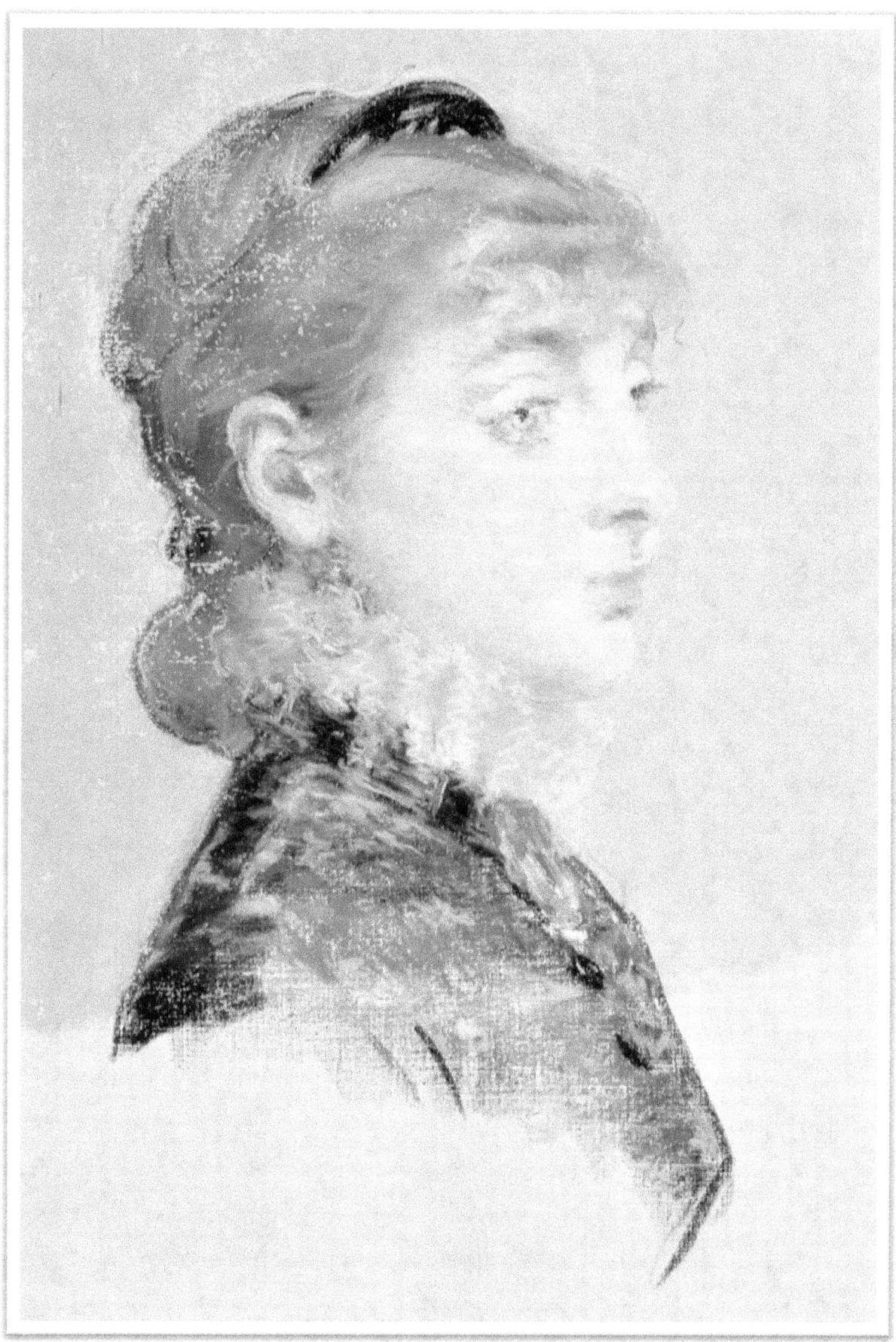

48. van Gogh, *The Rispal Restaurant at Asnières*

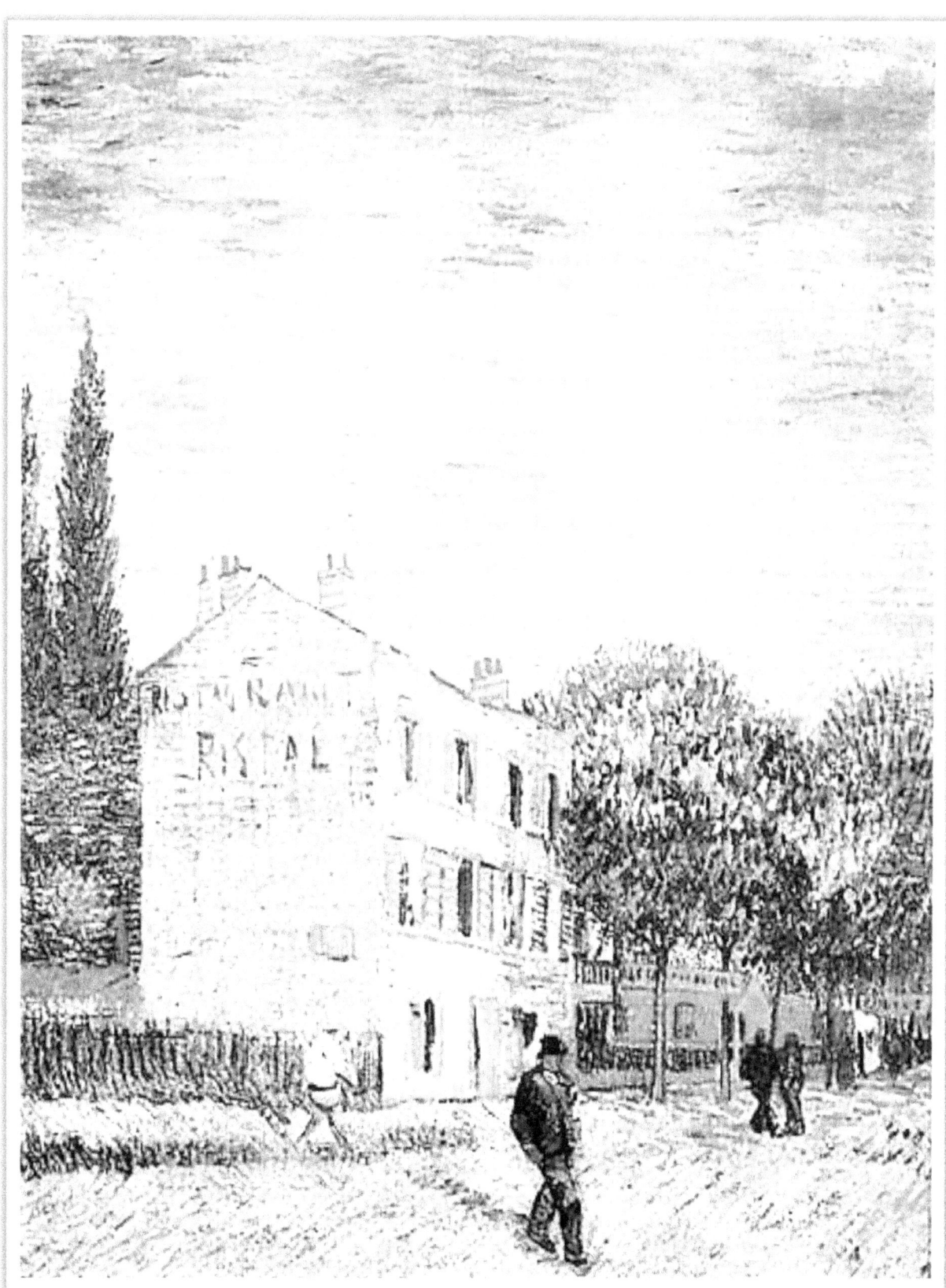

49. van Gogh, Wheat Field at Auvers with a White House

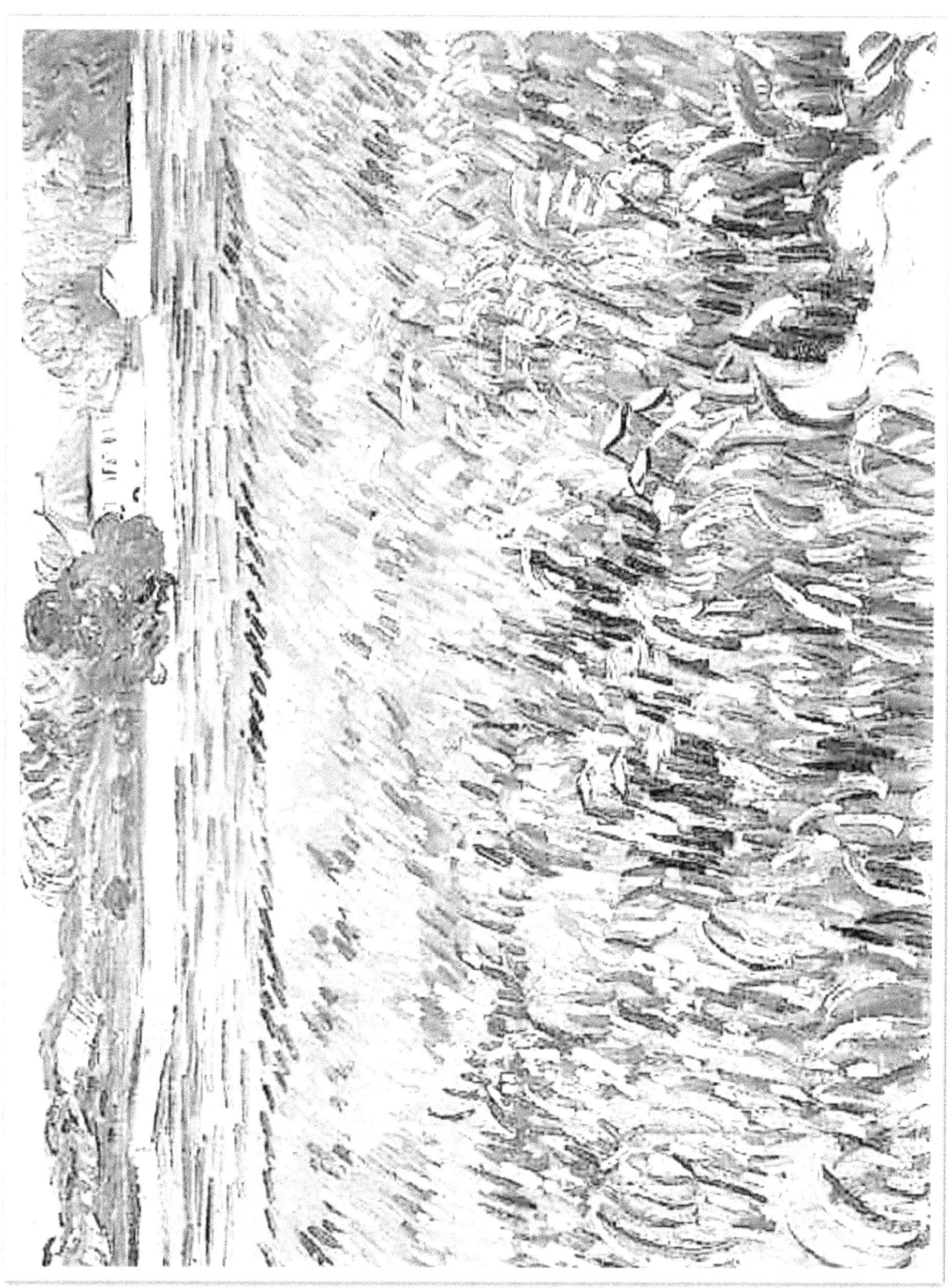

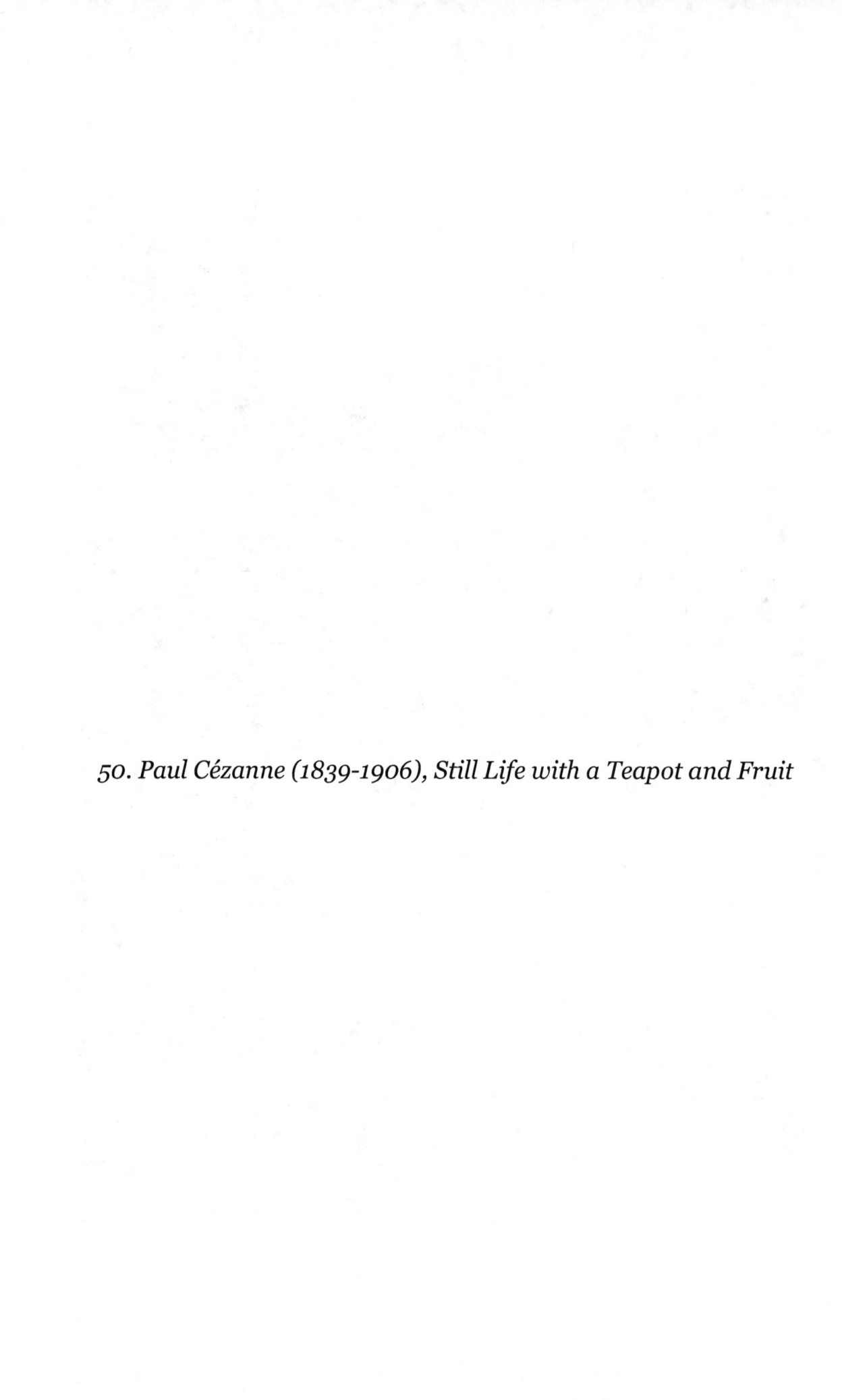

50. Paul Cézanne (1839-1906), Still Life with a Teapot and Fruit

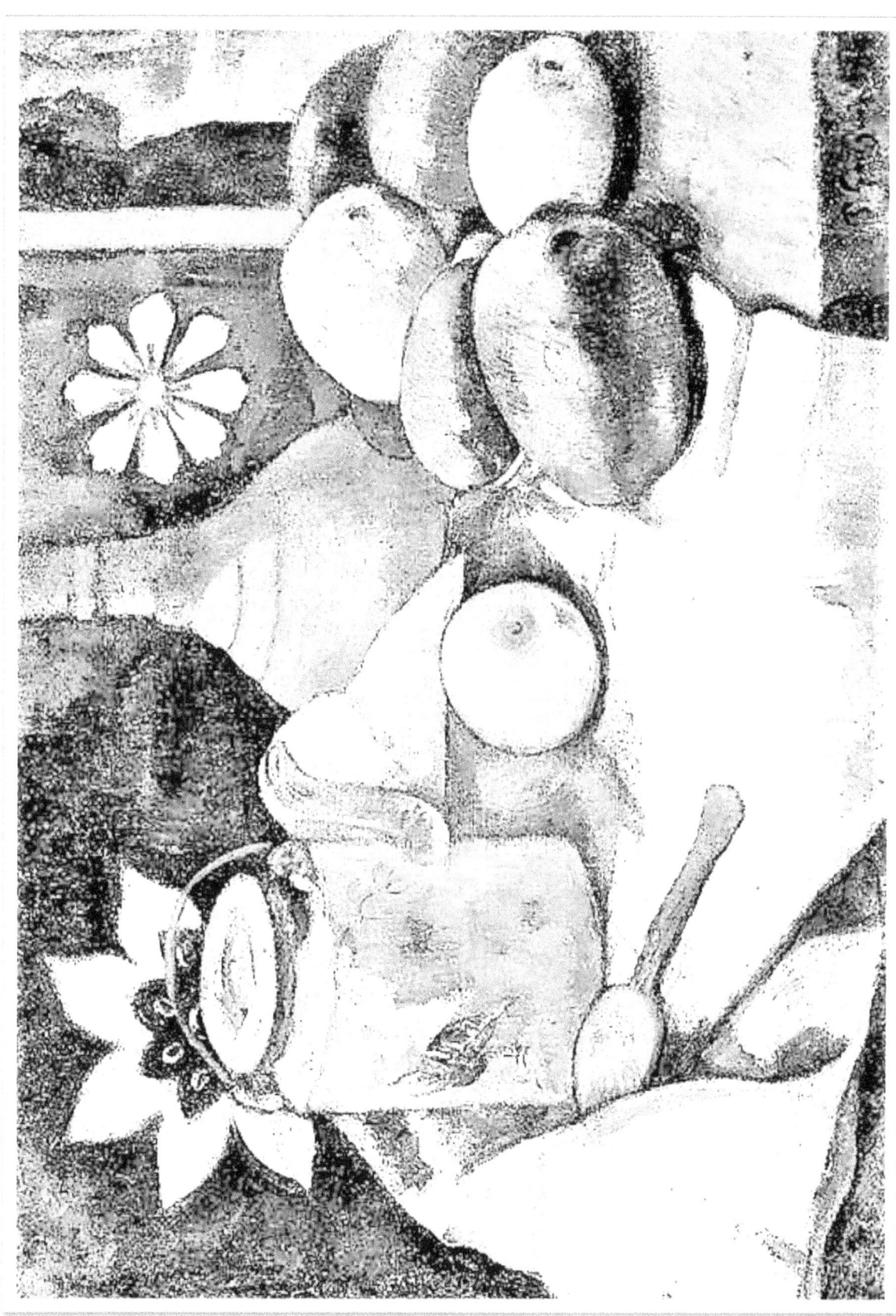

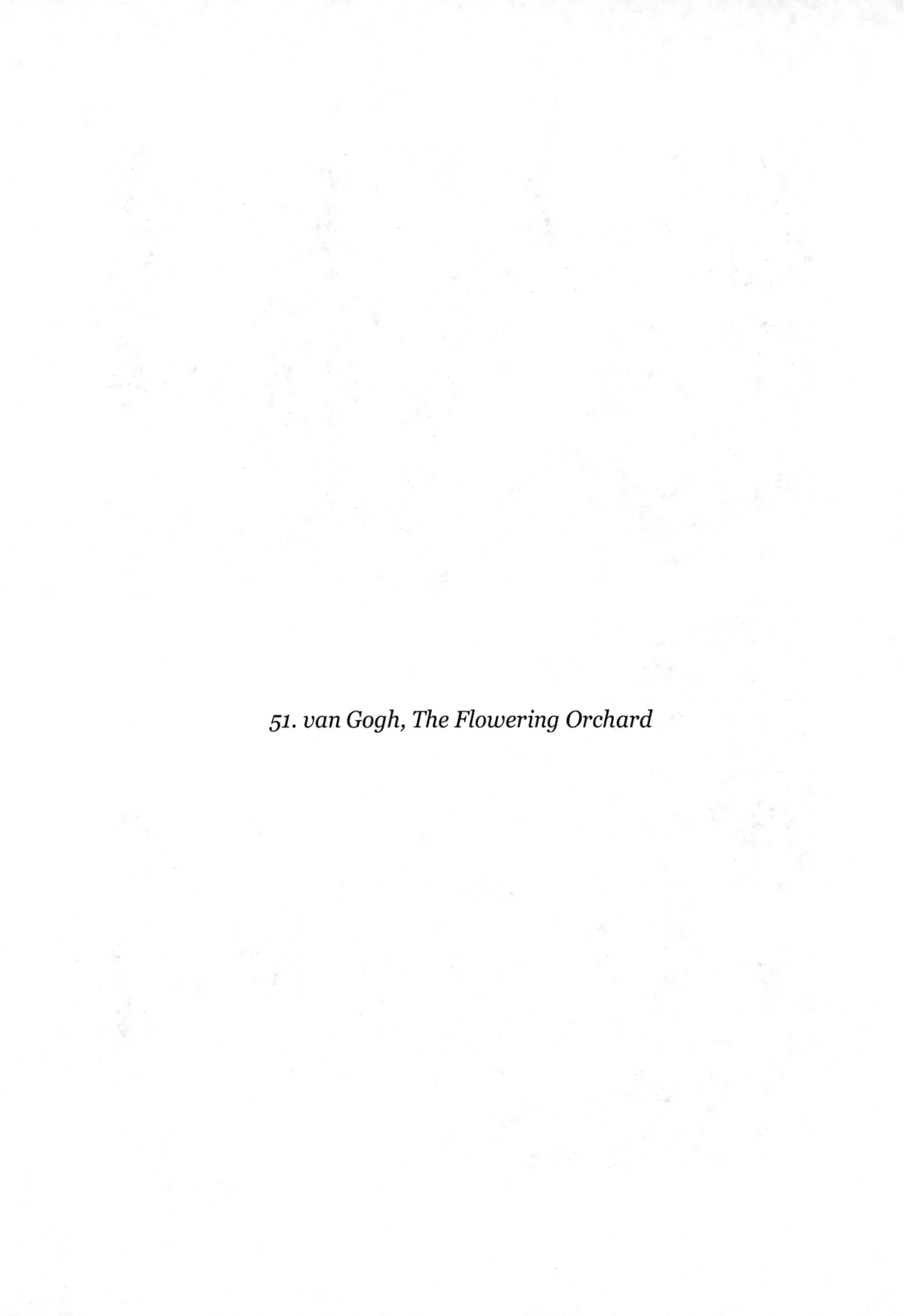

51. van Gogh, The Flowering Orchard

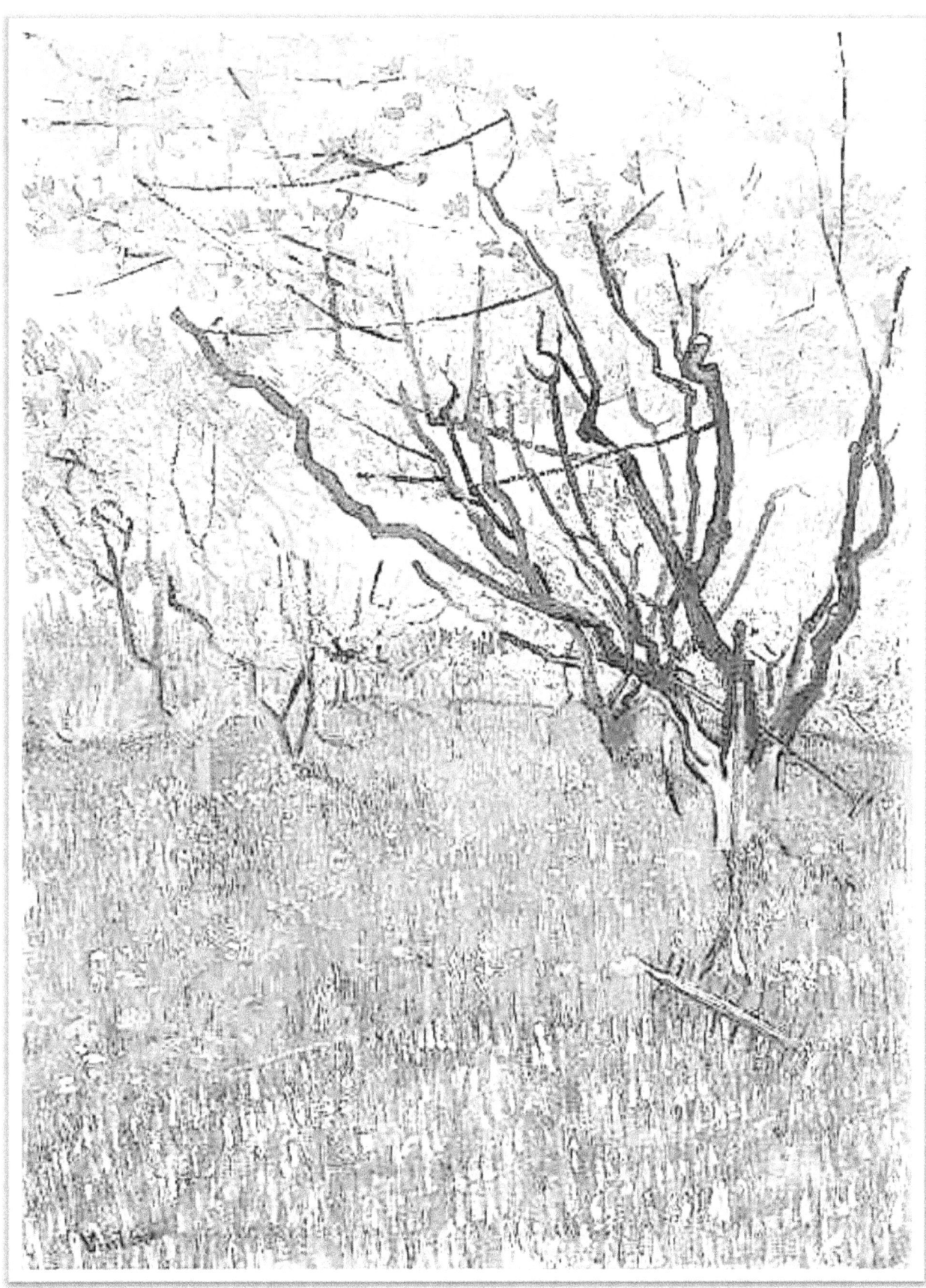

52. Lautrec, The White Horse "Gazelle"

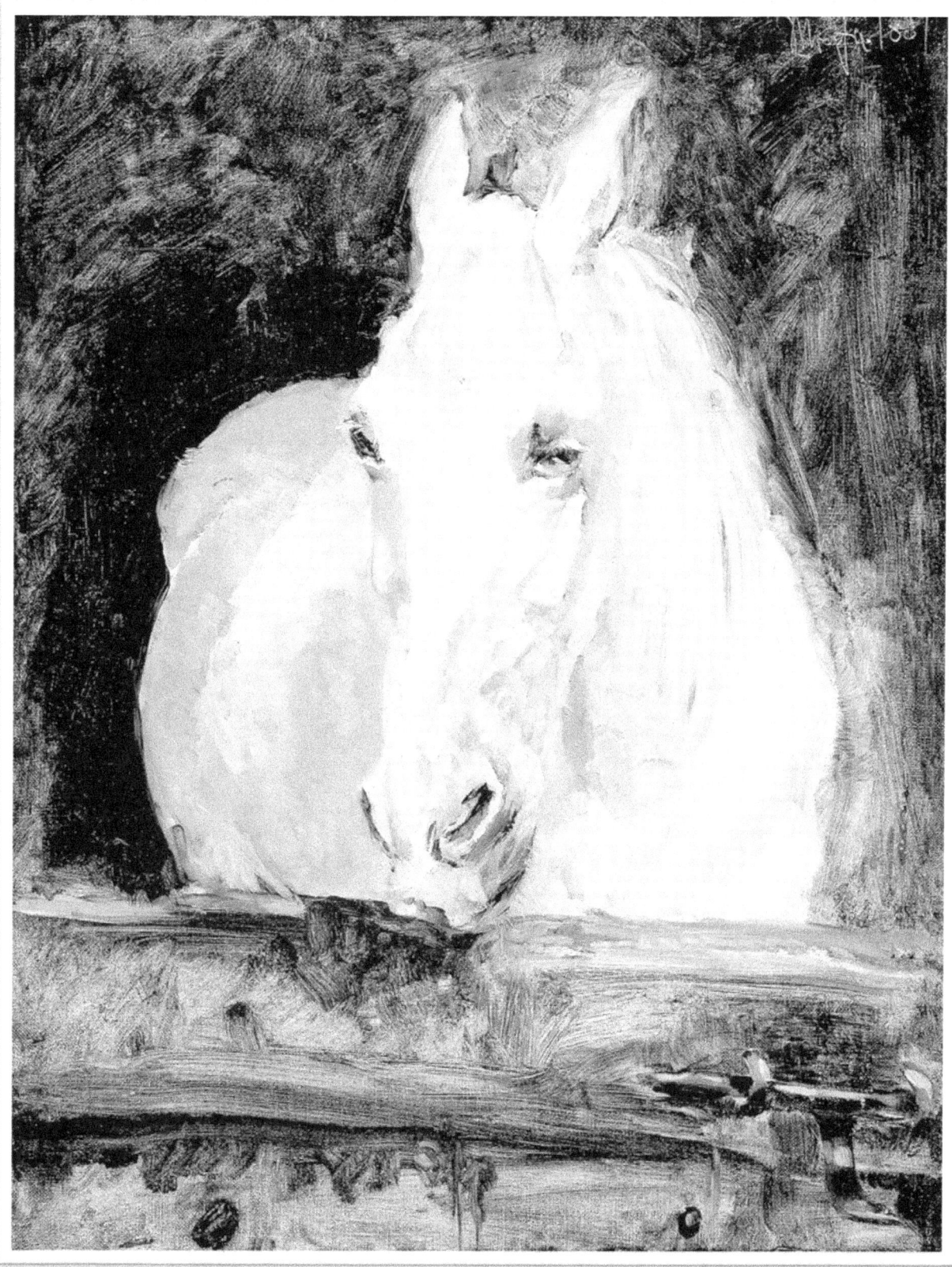

53. Manet, Boating

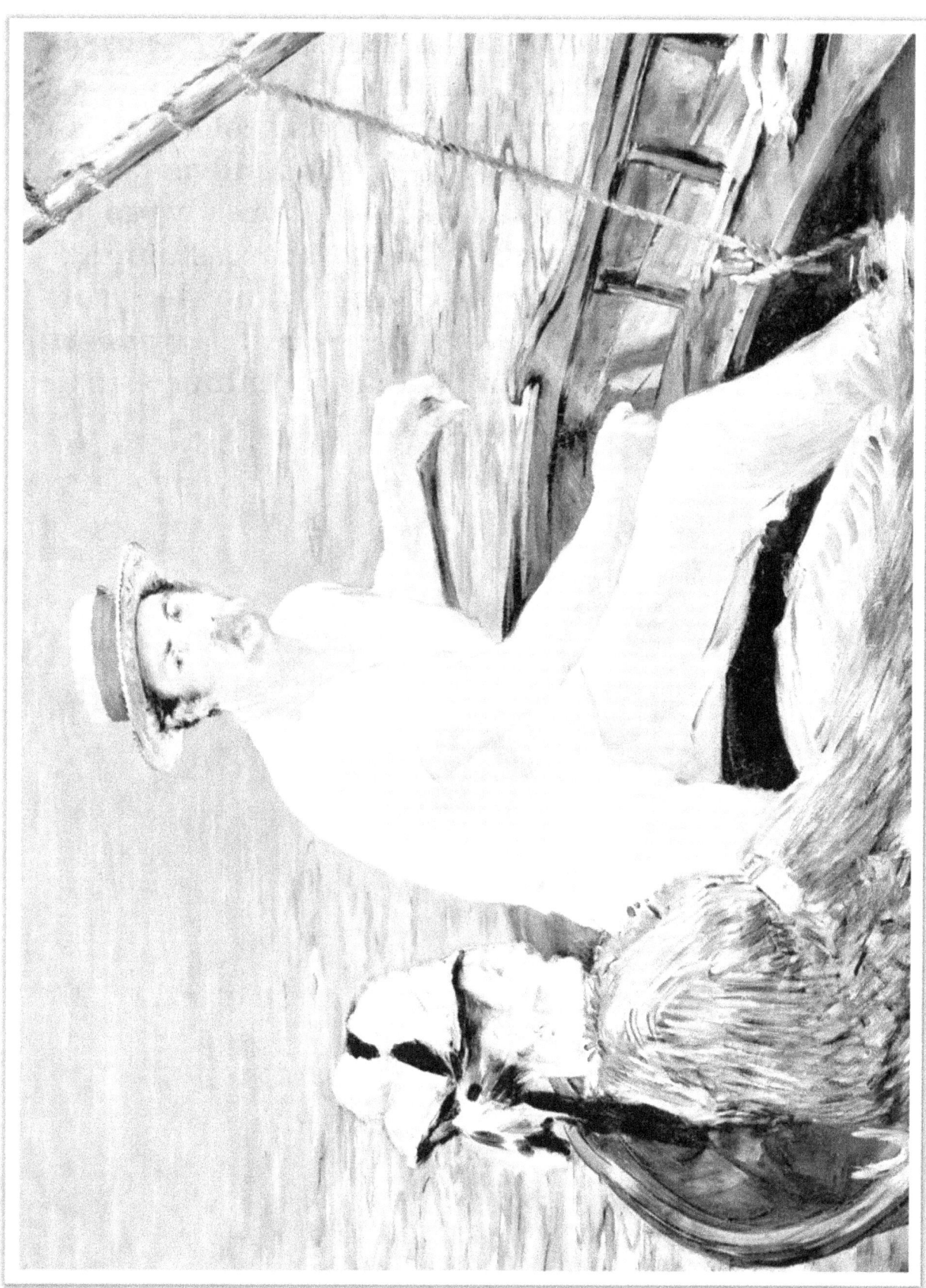

CREATIVE GRAYSCALE COLORING

is a new popular trend of the 21st century. It means you will ingeniously create your own work of art and a masterpiece to remember by applying color over a carefully optimized photo. The fantastic advantage of grayscale coloring is that the shading is already provided and it will show through your colors for a stunning outcome. So without any background knowledge of shading, it is possible for everyone to create a wonderful picture of great artistic depth with ease, enthusiasm and incredible fun.

l hope you enjoyed the artistic adventure and had great fun with it. You are kindly and warmly invited to write a comment about it on Amazon. Don't be shy and share your art on social media and Amazon as well. I would love to see your creations. That would be so nice and gratifying. Thank you. *IB*

For additional: izabella.creativeart@gmail.com

Post your creations on Facebook: Iza Bella Creative Art

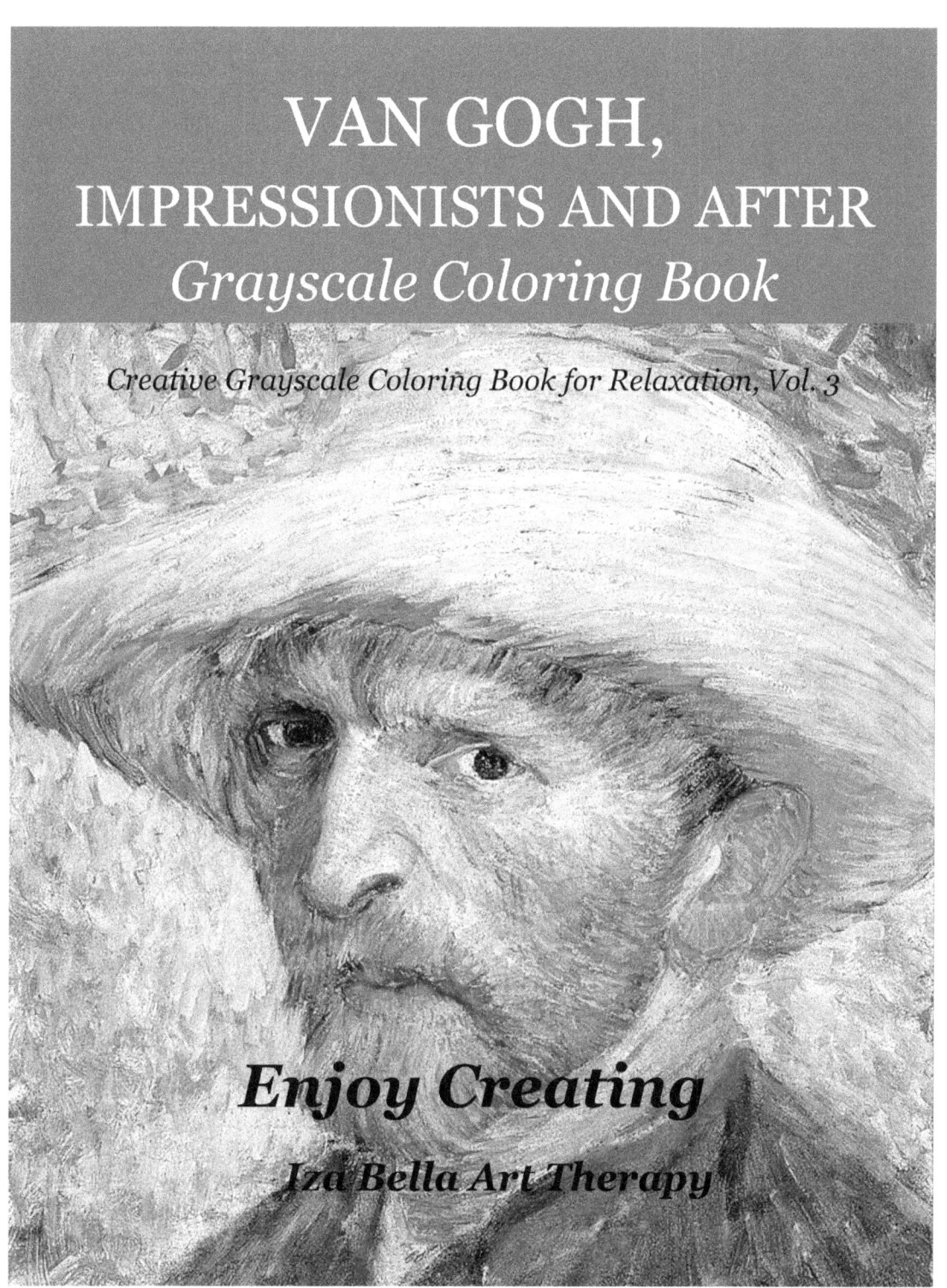

VAN GOGH,
IMPRESSIONISTS AND AFTER
Grayscale Coloring Book

Creative Grayscale Coloring Book for Relaxation, Vol. 3

Enjoy Creating

Iza Bella Art Therapy